The
Hay and Kington
Railways

by

GORDON RATTENBURY and RAY COOK

with 65 illustrations and 14 maps

RAILWAY & CANAL HISTORICAL SOCIETY

First published in 1996
by the Railway & Canal Historical Society
Registered office: Fron Fawnog, Hafod Road, Gwernymynydd, Mold, Clwyd CH7 5JS
Registered charity no.256047

ISBN 0 901461 19 9

Designed and typeset by
Malcolm Preskett
Printed in England by
Biddles Ltd, Guildford, Surrey

COVER ILLUSTRATION
The watercolour reproduced on the front cover was specially commissioned
from Edward Paget-Tomlinson for this publication. The scene is the Watton wharf
on the outskirts of Brecon in around 1820. This was the western terminus of the Hay Railway
where it formed a junction with the Brecknock & Abergavenny Canal. A train of coal, carried
up the canal by barge, is about to head off in the direction of Hay, while behind it a gang of
labourers are shovelling coal from the same barge into another row of waggons which,
no doubt, will head inland in due course. A herd of Herefords crosses the bridge,
apparently going home for milking from pastures on the south of the canal.
The bridge over the canal was built in the 1790s when the canal was constructed,
but the nearer bridge was only added in about 1812 when the Hay Railway was built.
On the bank above the railway a pile of damaged tramplates
and other scrap waits to be sold.

Contents

AUTHOR'S ACKNOWLEDGMENTS

One feels a certain trepidation in attempting to re-write and expand an existing work, particularly when one's original acquaintance with the subject came from the work concerned. My excuse for undertaking the present study is that in the course of investigating the histories of other tramroads a number of items concerning the Hay Railway have come to my notice. I must nevertheless record my indebtedness to Mr C. R. Clinker's work published in 1960.

Some years ago I learned that Mr Clinker was proposing to re-write and expand his original book and I passed to him much of the additional material that had come my way. But for his unfortunate death in April 1983 after a long period of ill health, I have no doubt that he would have included it in his new edition.

Whilst I have been responsible for the text, the maps are the work of Mr R. A. Cook who has brought the knowledge which he gained while accompanying Mr Clinker on his original fieldwork to bear on the subject to my great advantage.

Mr John van Laun has helped considerably by allowing me to use his published and unpublished work, and Mr John Norris has been to a great deal of trouble to help me with information concerning the early years of the Kington & Eardisley Railway.

The staffs of the former British Transport Historical Records Office in London; the Hereford & Worcester County Record Office, Hereford; the Hereford City Reference Library; Brecknock Museum, Brecon; Brecon Library and the National Library of Wales, Aberystwyth have all displayed great courtesy and patience in producing material for me to study, and what follows would have been impossible without their help.

Finally I must record my gratitude to the Managing Committee of the Railway & Canal Historical Society for their financial help with my out of pocket expenses.

Gordon Rattenbury, July 1987

ABBREVIATIONS

B&A	Brecknock & Abergavenny Canal
B&M	Brecon & Merthyr Railway
BBCo.	Brecknock Boat Company
HH&B	Hereford, Hay & Brecon Railway
K&E	Kington & Eardisley Railway
L&K	Leominster & Kington Railway
MCC	Monmouthshire Canal Company
MWR	Mid Wales Railway
WMR	Welsh Midland Railway

Foreword

AMONG the completed work left by the late Gordon Rattenbury when he died in 1990 were two related manuscripts, one on the Hay Railway, the other on the Kington Railway. They were accompanied by a series of maps, expertly drawn by Ray Cook to show the exact route of these two tramroads and to make it possible for the interested reader to follow their course on the ground. These maps had been revised under Gordon's guidance before, sadly, Ray also died in 1992. Between them, the text and the maps represented a substantial work on the history of these two early undertakings. The manuscripts and the maps were kindly made available to the Railway & Canal Historical Society by Gordon Rattenbury's son, John Rattenbury, with the concurrence of the late Mrs Enid Cook. The Society gladly accepted the opportunity of publishing what was seen as a valedictory volume to two faithful and active members of the Society. Both had been regular contributors to the Society's *Journal* and both had previously had work published by the Society in book form.

Together, these two iron railways, which were both worked by horse power, formed a main traffic artery in the Welsh border country many years before the steam locomotive became accepted as a reliable means of traction for use on similar lines. Its main function was the distribution of coal and iron from the Brecknock & Abergavenny Canal at Brecon northward to the towns of Hay (in the then County of Breconshire) and Kington (in Herefordshire), which made it unusual among such lines, as they were usually designed to bring traffic to a canal; beyond Kington a short extension to the Burlinjobb lime-works penetrated into Radnorshire. This line was built by two companies, the Hay Railway opened in sections between 1816 and 1818, and the Kington Railway which was opened to that town in 1820. They made an end-on junction at Eardisley. The form of track used was the plateway (now usually known as tramroad), employing L-section rails laid on stone blocks.

A feature of the combined line was its length of some 36 miles, at a time when few such lines exceeded about six miles, many being much shorter. The contemporary and nearby tramroad from Abergavenny to Hereford, owned by three companies, totalled only some 24 miles. The Stockton & Darlington Railway of 1825, which used steam locomotives extensively, had a main line of about 27 miles, while the Liverpool & Manchester Railway of 1830, which used locomotives almost throughout for both goods and passenger trains, was about 31 miles long. Even the Cromford & High Peak Railway, also of 1830, which used rope-worked inclines and horses, was only 34 miles long. So, in its day, the Hay/Kington line was, in terms of length at least, a major cross-country route and it seems that it was not until 1837 that it was eclipsed by the 78 miles of the Grand Junction Railway.

One feature of the line mirrored events of today. The companies were not empowered to act as carriers but simply owned and maintained the track, charging tolls for its use by haulage contractors or industrial owners. This was, in fact, the general method of operating public tramroads, and today we see the same principle adopted on British Railways for all classes of traffic.

Earlier accounts of the line have appeared, concentrating on one particular section or aspect of it, and all long out of print except for the most recent, in which the early tramroad is subsidiary to the railways which followed it. The present work expands and develops the work of another scholar of early railways, C. R. Clinker, whose *Hay Railway* had appeared in 1960. This was the first account of the Hay Railway to be based on primary records as available to the author at that time. The work of the present authors on the whole line in obscure contemporary documents, and its careful mapping by examination of the ground in conjunction with early plans, gives us a greatly enhanced picture of a once very useful line of rural transport which ensured a plentiful supply of coal to many small communities at a time when 'coal was King' but which had hitherto been at the mercy of the uncertain river Wye, never an easy navigation and only usable above Hereford in the winter months.

H. W. Paar

Editor's Introduction

AFTER the work of Gordon Rattenbury and Ray Cook had been accepted for publication by the Railway & Canal Historical Society, I was asked by the Publications Committee to prepare the manuscript for publication. My editorial work has extended no further than making what changes were needed to bring the text into line with the Society's house style. The substance is entirely that of the late author, while Ray Cook's maps remain in the state in which he left them. However, although I may not have made any major changes to the text, I have sought to complement it by means of further maps and illustrations, and at this point I would like to acknowledge the willing help which I have received from a number of individuals, both members and non-members of the R&CHS.

The illustration which appears on the front cover was prepared specially for this publication by Edward Paget-Tomlinson. His work can also be seen in the drawings which appear in various places within the text, the inclusion of which was his suggestion. Richard Dean has prepared the additional maps which appear within the text. Some of the photographs are the work of the authors of this book themselves, but these have been supplemented by the work of several additional contributors, to all of whom I am indebted. Stephen K. Jones made time to accompany me on an exploration of the line and to photograph many of the features which

still survive. Tim Edmonds has allowed me to use photographs which he had previously taken in Hereford City Museum for his own purposes. Stephen Duffell produced prints from Ray Cook's negatives, as did Hugh Compton from those of Bertram Baxter: both of these collections are now in the keeping of the Society. The latter also provided copies of prints from the C. R. Clinker collection, deposited by the Society in Brunel University Library. Original prints and documents have been reproduced by permission of Hereford & Worcester County Libraries, Hereford & Worcester County Record Office, the Brecknock Museum and the National Library of Wales. I am also grateful to various individuals and to Hereford City Museums for permission to include illustrations of artifacts in their possession.

Finally I would like to thank the Publications Committee of the Railway & Canal Historical Society for the opportunity of working on this text. I took the task on gladly as my own posthumous act of respect to the memory of Gordon Rattenbury, whose knowledge of the early tramroads of South Wales and whose enthusiasm for discovering all the details of their history were a constant cause for admiration, not only by myself but also by the many others whom he introduced to the study of early railways and tramroads.

Paul Reynolds
Swansea, August 1995

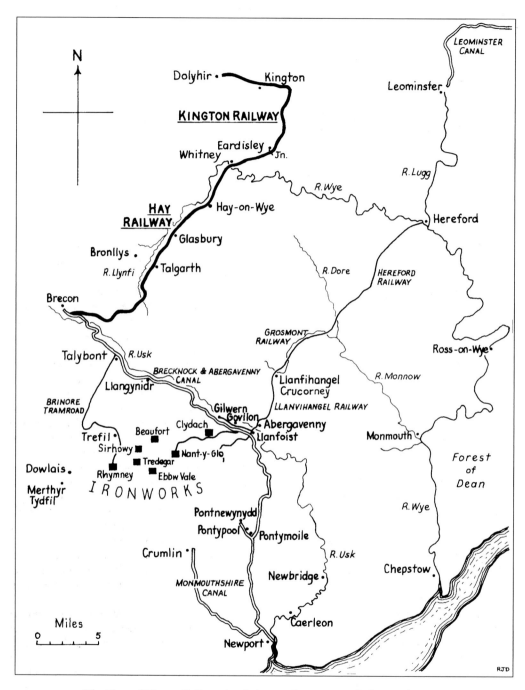

1. The Hay and Kington Railways in relation to other transport facilities in the region.
Map: R. J. Dean

CHAPTER ONE

THE HAY RAILWAY
Origins and Incorporation
(to 1811)

THE original plan of 1792 for what was to be known as the Abergavenny Canal envisaged a railroad from coal mines at Brynmawr down the Clydach valley to Gilwern. From here a canal was to run to Newbridge on Usk at the tidal limit of the river, whence river craft could carry the coal for shipment at the ancient port of Caerleon. Under the influence of the proprietors of the Monmouthshire Canal, who had obtained their Act that year, the southern terminal was changed to a junction at Pontymoile with the Pontypool branch of their canal.

The gentry of Brecon could see that if the canal could be extended westward from Gilwern to their town, they would be able to obtain coal more cheaply than by pack animals – the current mode of transport – and additionally they would be able to obtain some of the manufactured articles then becoming commonplace in England as the Industrial Revolution progressed. Thus it was that the Act that was obtained in March 1793 (33 Geo. III c.96) was for a canal from Brecon to Pontymoile under the title of the 'Brecknock & Abergavenny Canal'.[1]

At the time the city of Hereford and the western parts of Herefordshire obtained such coal as they used from collieries in the Forest of Dean. It was carried laboriously and expensively by boat up the river Wye. The difficulty with which the river was navigated can be judged from the fact that only in times of flood was it passable by fully laden boats, and with no towing path haulage had

to be by teams of men. In spite of these difficulties the river was considered to be navigable as far up as Hay.

The prospect of the canal as far as Brecon quickly suggested extensions which might usefully be constructed. At a meeting held on 11 June 1793, only a month after the inaugural meeting of the B&A, it was proposed that a canal should be made from Brecon to Whitney on Wye, with the object of supplying coal from Monmouthshire to western Herefordshire. The plan was approved and £47,000 was subscribed at the meeting.[2] The notice of intent, published in the *Hereford Journal* on 11 September, showed that the proposed Brecon, Hay & Whitney Canal would leave the B&A near the 'intended aqueduct' over the Usk at Brynich and enter the Wye 'at or near to a place called Whitney'. There seems to have been a rapid falling off in enthusiasm. On 1 May 1794 letters were despatched to all subscribers detailing the amounts due from each towards the costs that had been incurred for the survey and for the meetings that had been held. The plan was then shelved, as were so many others in the years of the 'canal mania'.[3]

The B&A opened in stages from Gilwern to Brecon, which was reached on 24 December 1800.[4] In an attempt to initiate traffic on their canal, the B&A tried for several years to enter the sale coal trade on their own account, but steadily increasing charges made for the coal by their sole supplier, Edward Kendall of the Beaufort Iron-works, led to the trade being handed over to a consortium of their own committee consisting of Jeffreys Wilkins (their banker), John Powell (their solicitor), John Peirce and John Lloyd, all of Brecon, who came to be known by the collective title of 'the Boat Company'. Probably they were the only carriers on the canal for some years, and at the B&A general meeting on 25 April 1799, a vote of thanks was passed for their efforts in establishing a trade on the canal. The partnership was formalised by a deed in January 1805, designating the company as 'The Brecknock Boat Company' or 'Wilkins, Lloyd, Powell & Peirce'.[5]

The next attempt at providing communication between Brecon and western Herefordshire was announced in a news paragraph in *The Cambrian* of 9 March 1805, which stated that a subscription had been opened at the Brecon Bank of Wilkins & Co. 'for the purpose of ascertaining the most eligible level for a railroad from the Monmouth and Brecon Canal to the river Wye', prophetically giving the canal the name that was

assumed in 1865 after the amalgamation of the B&A and Monmouthshire Canals!

A survey was made, and on 15 and 29 May notices appeared in the *Hereford Journal* calling a meeting on 6 June at the *Swan Inn*, Hay of those willing to promote the Hay Tram Road. The notices were signed by six Brecon businessmen, including Jeffreys Wilkins and John Lloyd of the BBCo. No notice of intent to apply for an Act has been found, nor has any copy of the plan been seen. It is only known from a later scheme that the plan was drawn by Thomas Cartwright, who was working for the B&A at the time.[6] Once again no progress was made and the scheme lapsed.

No further suggestion was made for communication northward from Brecon for the next five years until, on 25 July 1810, a notice appeared in the *Hereford Journal* under the heading 'Herefordshire and Breconshire Rail Road' calling a meeting for the following day at the *Swan Inn*, Hay 'for the purpose of taking into consideration

2. *Swan Inn,* Hay. The meeting of 26 July 1810 at which it was agreed to seek powers for the construction of the Hay Railway was held here, as were subsequent meetings of the committee and of the proprietors. The original is from an anonymous 'Sketches on a Tour through Wales' of 1808.
By permission of the National Library of Wales

3. *Swan Hotel*, Hay. The *Swan Inn* was acquired by Sir Charles Morgan in around 1816 and was rebuilt as the Swan Hotel in 1821. Hay Railway meetings continued to be held here.
Photo: Stephen K. Jones (1994)

a TRAM or RAIL ROAD from the Brecon and Abergavenny Canal to communicate with Herefordshire, Radnorshire and the north-western part of Breconshire. It was signed by seventeen influential landowners, Members of Parliament and bankers, including three members of the BBCO. – Jeffreys Wilkins, John Lloyd and Walter Powell, who was acting in his capacity as executor of the will of John Powell. The scheme must already have been under consideration for some time, since on 2 July John Peirce, acting in the name of Wilkins, Lloyd & Co., had purchased for £900 a plot of land adjacent to the canal at Brynich. It lay in such a position that it would also have abutted onto the suggested line of the tramroad – on the face of it an excellent investment, giving wharves on both tramroad and canal! [7]

The *Hereford Journal* of 1 August carried a report of the meeting of 26 July. The meeting agreed that the construction of a tramroad from the canal to Parton Cross, near Eardisley, would be beneficial to the adjoining country. It was

resolved to obtain a re-survey of the route proposed by Cartwright with a fresh estimate of the probable cost. A committee of twelve was appointed, any three of whom should constitute a quorum. In ordering that a subscription list should be opened at the Brecon Bank, the somewhat unusual proviso was included that every subscription of £1 or more should entitle the subscriber to the option of taking up one £100 share for each £1 subscribed; but it also permitted the withdrawal of any name on the forfeiture of the £1 paid so long as notice of intention was given before the general meeting which was to held to receive the surveyor's report. Any subscriber not giving notice was to be held liable to take up the appropriate number of shares.

It was reported to the B&A committee on 23 August that the chairman had received a letter from James Spencer, a Hay solicitor, writing on behalf of the provisional tramroad committee, requesting that William Crosley, the B&A's engineer, might be permitted to make a survey for them. In view of the trade which the canal company thought might accrue to them, a resolution was immediately passed

> … that this Committee feeling great pleasure in complying with their request, do grant their Surveyor permission to take in such survey as soon as his present duty will, with convenience, allow. [8]

Notice of the intention of the promoters to apply to Parliament for an Act appeared in the *Hereford Journal* of 5 September 1810. It stated that the intended line would commence on the canal at Brynych and pass through the parishes of Llanhamlach, Llandew, Talachddy, Llanvillo, Llandevalley, Talgarth, Broynllis, Aberlunvay, Glasbury, Llanigon, Hay, Llewes, Clyro, Bettws Clyro, Cussop, Hardwick, Clifford, Willey, Whitney, Winforton, Willersley and Eardisley. It would terminate in Eardisley. The notice was dated 20 August 1810 and must have been prepared before Crosley's plan, which was dated September 1810, had been received.[9]

The *Hereford Journal* of 7 November reported on a meeting which had been held on 26 October to consider Crosley's plan and estimate. The report stated that a single road could be made for £42,000, which would include sufficient land for doubling the track in future, if this should be found to be necessary. Tonnages for upward carriage should realise £5,918 annually and return tonnages £1,479. The committee estimated that repairs would cost £1,000 per annum, but to be on the safe side put it at £1,379, which would leave an annual profit of £6,000. It was thought that, by the tramroad, coal could be sold at Hay for 21 shillings per ton, and at Parton Cross for 24 shillings. The meeting resolved that £42,000 would be enough to cover the cost of construction and that a subscription should be opened. This would not be binding on the signatories unless £35,000 should be received by 1 February 1811. Bankers in Brecon and Kington should be requested to receive subscriptions.

Crosley's report and the committee's comments thereon were printed and circulated on 1 December 1810. There are slight differences in the amounts shown by Crosley and those published in the report of the meeting. Crosley estimated the cost of the line 'Formed for a Double Road but laid Single … £41,000. A Double Road completed … £60,250'. He considered that repairs and other costs should be only £800 per annum. Whilst he had made the survey from Brynich, he thought that 'the most desirable line is from Brecon'. In their comments the committee stated that the completion of the canal to Newport was imminent, and that the tramroad would make available 'Slate, Iron, Tar, Bristol Goods, and all others that are bulky in proportion to their value' in addition to coal, and that return loads of grain, cider, apples and bark would be carried, but they admitted the impossibility of estimating accurately what quantities would be involved. It is interesting to note the places from which western Herefordshire was obtaining its coal at the time:

> At present coal is Fifteen Shillings per ton at Brecon, and being of the strongest quality, a Ton is fully equal to Thirty Cwt. of Clee Hill, and Two Tons of Sousnat Coal * … The use of Coal in preference to Wood is everywhere gaining ground.[10]

A general meeting of those who must now be termed subscribers was held on 12 December 1810. It was resolved to depute Hugh Bold, a Brecon solicitor, and Edward Frere, a partner in the Clydach Ironworks near Gilwern, both of whom were on the B&A committee, to acquaint that committee 'with the nature and scope of this undertaking'.[11] The canal company's meeting of 18 December considered the proposed tramroad and resolved that it appeared that it would be of great advantage to their concern. They ordered that their Clerk should forward copies of the tramroad company's statement and Crosley's plans to all members of their Monmouthshire and Breconshire committees for consideration at the joint meeting to be held in January. The joint meeting, which took place on 11 January 1811, confirmed the views previously expressed and ordered that all shareholders should be circularised to that effect.

---

* Clee Hill is five miles east of Ludlow, Shropshire. Sousnat is Southnet, Worcestershire, twelve miles north-east of Leominster. Coal from this source would have been carried by road and the then incomplete Leominster Canal.

On 13 January Thomas Bold, Hugh's brother, informed Sir Charles Morgan, who had large landed interests around Brecon, that the subscription for the tramroad was filling well.[12] At a meeting of subscribers held on 18 January it was reported that £31,600 had already been received and a further £3,400 was underwritten at the meeting. It was resolved that the provisional committee 'to forward the general purposes of the undertaking' should consist of all subscribers of £500 or over, any three of whom should form a quorum.[13] A printed list of subscribers, forwarded by James Spencer to Morgan on 9 February, showed that to date £45,600 was available, and an endorsement in ink added that another £2,000 had been promised.[14] The *Hereford Journal* of 13 February 1811 reported that £51,300 had been subscribed.

A petition to the House of Commons for leave to present a Bill in accordance with the notice of intent of August 1810 was lodged on 1 February 1811, and the Bill received its first reading on 19 February – a day before its contents were revealed to the subscribers! [15] Possibly the intention was to keep from the B&A subscribers for as long as possible the fact that the Bill contained a clause that would reduce the canal company's powers under their Act of 1793 to make roads, railroads or canals to any manufacturing or extractive industry lying within eight miles of the canal.

William Powell, the canal company's solicitor, noticed it, however, and on 23 February he wrote to all members of the Monmouthshire committee to inform them of its effect, pointing out that a similar clause might be incorporated in the Bill shortly to be presented for the Llanvihangel Railway. As the Hay Bill was due to go to the Committee of the House on 20 March it was essential that the canal company should hold a special general meeting before that date. Powell stated that he intended to call this meeting for 13 March. He apologised to the Monmouthshire members for calling it during the sitting of their Assize (always a social occasion), but he trusted that it would not interfere too much with their arrangements.[16]

The Monmouthshire committee of the B&A met on 6 March when Hugh Bold explained the reasons for holding the meeting on 13 March, which were accepted. The special general meeting heard that the promoters of the Hay Railway were proposing that the B&A should waive their right to make a tramroad in the direction of Hay, but it was decided not to oppose the clause when it was learned that the waiver was intended to be limited to three years. The general meeting of 25 April confirmed the decision.

Other moves were afoot, however, and on 6 March several persons interested in the B&A petitioned the Commons that the logical place for the tramroad to terminate was at the canal wharf at the Watton, Brecon, and not at Brynich.[17] On 7 March, Thomas Bold advised Morgan that the proposed alteration to the site of the terminus would involve a considerable tract of his land, and that one of his tenants considered that he would be seriously inconvenienced by such a move.[18] On 10 March, Bold informed Morgan that Spencer had called on him the previous day asking his consent for the tramroad to pass over a piece of land that he rented from Morgan, to which he had replied that he would have to be governed by Morgan's reaction to the proposal, and that other tenants had given Spencer the same answer. Bold's letter concluded:

… I am fearful the engineer, Mr. Crossley [*sic*] has not consulted the convenience of the Landlord or Tenant … which I think he might.[19]

Nobody seems to have brought up the point that all cargoes destined to be carried on the Hay Railway would have to pay the B&A one and a half miles more in tonnages!

The Bill received its second reading on 18 March, and on the following day the Hay committee reported that all landowners affected by the proposed line to Brecon had assented to the change. On 5 April permission was given for new plans to be deposited.[20] The 'new' plan, annotated to the effect that it showed

… the intended variation to go from the Public Wharf of the Brecon & Abergavenny Canal near Brecon instead of Brynich …

is still dated September 1810.[21] Public notice of the intended alterations was given in the *Hereford Journal* of 10 April, quoting the names of the land-

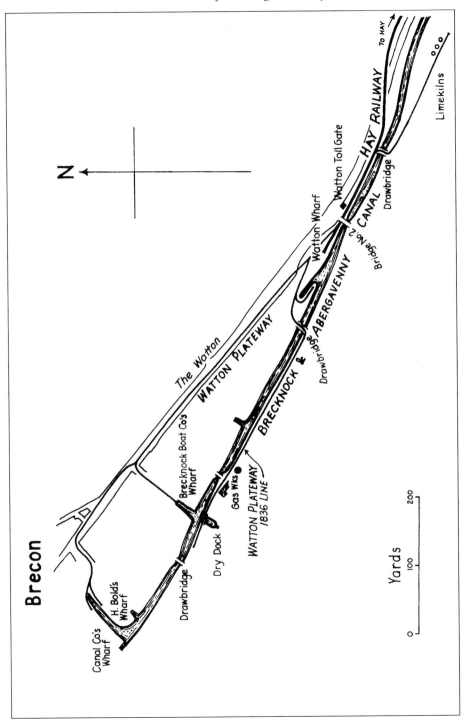

4. The Brecknock & Abergavenny Canal at Brecon, showing the location of the southern terminus of the Hay Railway at the Watton wharf. (Based on J. Wood's 'Plan of Brecknock', 1834, with the 1836 tramroad taken from the deposited plans of the Breconshire Railway & Canal, 1858). Map: R. J. Dean

AN

A C T

For making and maintaining a Railway or Tram Road, from or near the Public Wharf of the *Brecknock* and *Abergavenny* Canal, in the Parish of *Saint John the Evangelist*, in the County of *Brecon*, to or near to a certain Place called *Parton Cross*, in the Parish of *Eardisley*, in the County of *Hereford*.

WHEREAS the Turnpike Roads in the Neighbour- Preamble hood of the Town of *Hay*, in the County of *Brecon*, have been greatly injured and destroyed by Carriages travelling thereon, laden with Coals, Corn, and other heavy Commodities, which are carried to and from the *Brecknock and Abergavenny Canal* and the adjoining Counties of *Hereford* and *Radnor*, and owing to the constant Draught of such heavy Commodities thereon, are now in a very dilapidated and ruinous State, and cannot be kept in repair, even at enormous Expence: And whereas the making and maintaining of a Railway or Tram Road from the said Canal through the several Townships, Parishes, and Places hereinafter mentioned, to or near to a certain Place called *Parton Cross*, in the Parish of *Eardisley*, in the County of *Hereford*, would not only greatly relieve such Roads from the Damage they sustain, but the Carriage and Conveyance of the aforesaid Commodities would be most materially facilitated and cheapened, and the Trade and Communication between the adjoining Counties very considerably increased; by all which means the said Undertaking will tend greatly to improve the Value of Lands and Estates near the said Railway

A   01

5. The Hay Railway's Act of Incorporation (51 Geo. III c.122, 25 May 1811): the first page of the text of the Act. By permission of Hereford and Worcester County Libraries

owners and occupiers concerned, and on 24 April the B&A gave permission for the tramroad to pass through their land at the Watton. The Bill received its third reading on 14 May and was then passed to the Lords, where it passed all its stages by 21 May. It received the Royal Assent on 25 May 1811.[22]

The Act was a typical tramroad Act of the period. It authorised a capital of £50,000 in shares of £100, with borrowing powers of £15,000 which might be raised by the issue of further shares, promissory notes, or by mortgage of the undertaking. Owners of adjoining lands were to be allowed to make branches from the main line to their own property and to establish wharves, and they were to be able to pass along the tramroad within the limits of their own land toll-free. Where public roads were crossed the flange of the plates was not to stand proud of the road surface by more than one inch. It was assumed in the Act that the tramroad company would make its own crossing of the Wye at Whitney, and section 91 specified that only the company's servants and those in charge of waggons should be permitted to cross the river by the company's bridge: other persons were to be obliged to use the existing toll-bridge. Should any other than those engaged in tramroad business cross the company's bridge, they were to incur a penalty of 20s to be paid to the proprietors of the toll-bridge. This was also to apply should the company adopt any other means of crossing the river, such as a ferry.

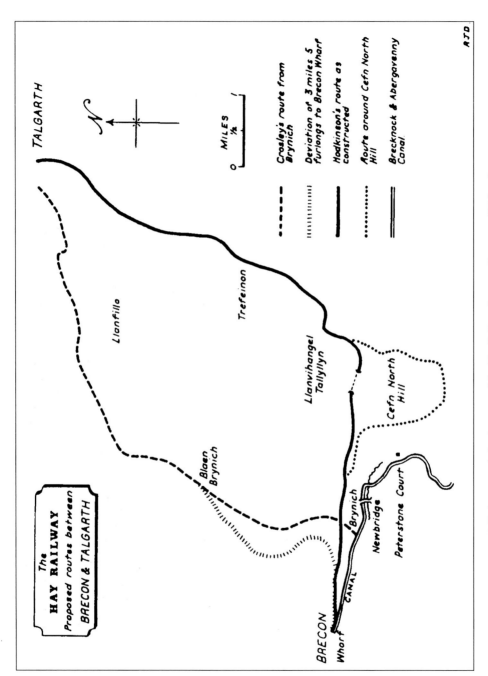

6. Early proposals for the route of the Hay Railway between Brecon and Talgarth.
Map: R. J. Dean

CHAPTER TWO

THE HAY RAILWAY
Start of Construction
(1811 – 1812)

It appears that very soon doubts were being expressed as to the suitability of Crosley's line. A notice in the *Hereford Journal* of 10 July 1811 called a general meeting of subscribers for 22 July and included a request for the services of

… any engineer willing to undertake the re-survey of the above Railway as soon as the harvest is over and make proper Estimates and Sections …

Any interested party was to send particulars of his proposals to Spencer and to attend the committee meeting on 31 July at the *Swan Inn,* Hay with testimonials of his qualifications. Also required was a person competent to undertake the position of agent to supervise the construction of the line and to act as 'Pay Clerk' (i.e. clerk of the works) to the company. Any applicant for this post was also requested to attend the same meeting, prepared to provide sureties for his good faith.

The committee, composed of those who had subscribed for £500 or more shares, was elected at the general meeting, and immediately afterwards ordered that a call of £10 per share, payable in two instalments of £5, should be made, payments due before 13 September.[23]

John Hodgkinson (a cousin of Benjamin Outram, the tramroad and canal engineer of Butterley Ironworks), who had recently completed the Sirhowy Tramroad in Monmouthshire was probably the only contender for the job of re-surveying the Hay Railway, and on 31 July the committee engaged him at a fee of £65. He was given orders to 'mark out the path of the Road with pegs' and to report to the committee on 7 September with sections and estimates of his proposals. The same day the committee considered a letter from Crosley demanding payment for his survey, but his request was refused on the grounds that he had not yet supplied them with sections of his line: possibly it was this omission which made a re-survey necessary, since until these were to hand it was not known what gradients he proposed to adopt.

After appointing William Williams of the Brecon Bank to be their Treasurer and authorising payment to James Spencer of £1,000, his fees for obtaining the Act, the meeting decided to advertise for 2,000 tons of tramplates, 'to be made of good strong bodied grey iron and to the Cheltenham Rail Road pattern weighing not exceeding 50 pounds per plate'.[24] They were to be delivered at the rate of 100 tons per month, 1,600 tons at Brecon and 400 tons at 'Broynliss' (Bronllys), the manufacturers to make good any breakages occurring within twelve months of the tramroad being opened. The committee reserved to themselves the right to alter the type of plate.

The advertisement appeared in the *Hereford Journal* of 7 August 1811, when the spelling of Bronllys suffered a further mutation to 'Bronhurst'! After detailing the company's requirements for plates, it went on to state that at their meeting on 14 September the committee would consider proposals for the construction of the tramroad from one or more persons, and that plans and sections of the line would be available at Spencer's office in Hay six days before the meeting.

7. Complete length of tramplate from the Hay Railway,
found at Llwynau Bach and now preserved in the hotel bar.
Photo: Stephen K. Jones (1994) by permission of Mr A. Reynolds

The various tenders for the tramplates were examined by the committee on 17 August. They varied considerably from the tender of Bailey & Wayne of Nantyglo Ironworks at £6 16s 6d per ton for 800 tons delivered at Brecon to that of Benjamin Hall of Rhymney Ironworks who proposed to charge £7 17s 6d per ton for 500 tons delivered at Brecon. The committee decided to accept Bailey & Wayne's offer, and also that of Frere, Cooke & Co. of Clydach Ironworks for 800 tons delivered at Brecon at £6 19s 0d per ton and 400 tons at Bronllys at £7 10s 0d per ton. The total quantity of plates ordered would have been sufficient to lay 25½ miles of track, and would have sufficed to lay Crosley's line of 23 miles 2 furlongs and all passing places.

Hodgkinson reported to the committee on 7 September suggesting two possible new routes. He was critical of Crosley's line on the grounds that the rise of 309 feet from Brecon was excessive, and the fall from Blaen Brynich to Parton Cross of 525 feet on gradients varying from 1:71 to 1:1584 was too irregular for easy working. By Hodgkinson's reckoning one horse would have been able to haul only one ton over the summit in either direction at a cost of £3 9s per ton for the whole distance. He estimated that it would cost £52,743 18s to construct, some £16,500 more than Crosley's estimate! In his report Hodgkinson stated that he would have preferred to have started his line at Newbridge (Brynich) but as his instructions had been to plan a line starting at the Watton wharf he had accordingly planned two routes from Brecon, one of 26 miles 1 furlong which passed to the south of Cefn North Hill (SO 103268) before turning north, the other two miles shorter and passing through a tunnel near Llanvihangel Talyllyn (SO 105275). His preference was for the longer line which climbed 154 feet from the Watton by a gradient of 1:158, which he estimated to cost £50,375 12s.[25] The tunnel line would have to climb more steeply and would reach a summit of 188 feet above the Watton at a cost of £52,743 18s.[26] On either of his lines Hodgkinson estimated that the cost of haulage for the whole distance would be 2s 5d per ton. At the northern end of the line he proposed that the terminus should be in Eardisley village (SO 313489) instead of at Parton Cross (SO 313483).

The meeting of 7 September decided to call a general meeting for 30 September. In order to give the shareholders ample time to consider the proposed variation of the route, the committee decided on the text of the Parliamentary notice to be inserted in the *Hereford Journal* on 11, 18 and 25 September. Strangely, this only mentioned a line through 'an archway or tunnel' and ignored the line around the hill. It did, however, give the intention to terminate at Eardisley village.

The committee made several further decisions at the same meeting. Crosley was to be paid £180 in full for his services. They would employ David Davies of Llangattock to make a valuation of the land that would be required in Breconshire and Benjamin Wanewright of Hereford to do the same for the land within his county. A further call of £10 per share was made, due on 25 October. Spencer was to find land on which the tramplates might be stored and scales and weights should be provided at Bronllys to weigh the plates delivered there – as Hodgkinson's line did not touch the place, the choice of location seems rather strange.

Hodgkinson appears to have convinced the general meeting on 30 September that his route around Cefn North Hill was to be preferred, as the printed copy of his original proposals, issued over that date, contains a copy of the resolution that was then passed, stating that the line around the hill was to be specified in the forthcoming Bill, and not the tunnel line described in the notice of 11 September. In the meantime it was intended to proceed with construction on those parts of the line that were covered by the existing Act.[27]

The committee met on the same day and were faced with a request from the Clydach Ironworks for payment for 15 tons of plates delivered at Brecon and 90 tons at Bronllys. As scales and weights had not yet been provided there was no means of checking these quantities, so it was ordered that they should be paid £700 on account. Hodgkinson was instructed to liaise with the iron company to find a more suitable place at which the plates should be delivered in future, Bronllys now being off the proposed line, so as to save on transport expenses. Spencer, who was paid £500 on account of moneys that he had expended for the company, was instructed to apply to the owners of the land through which Hodgkinson's line was to pass to obtain their consent, and Hodgkinson was instructed to mark out the line

from Fforddfawr (SO 192397) to Eardisley and was paid his fee for the survey and report, £60.

By 8 November Hodgkinson was able to report that he had marked out part of his line, and that

… between Sheephouse [SO 211415] and Stow [SO 282471, now known as Stowe] the line will keep within the distance allowed by the Act of Parliament excepting through the land of Mrs Judith Parsons and Tomkyns Dew Esquire.

Spencer was instructed to obtain their consents and to have the land valued, and in order to avoid cluttering the committee business a sub-committee was appointed to negotiate for land 'with or without fences'. A further payment on account of £800 to the Clydach Ironworks was ordered, and the landlord of the *Swan Inn* was paid £39 for the cost of the meetings held there. The committee heard that there were a number of defaulters on the first call due the previous September, and Spencer, as Clerk, was ordered to write to those concerned. As solicitor, he was instructed to prepare the draft of the forthcoming Bill which would be needed to authorise the change of route and of the northern terminal. It was ruled that in future the chair would be taken at meetings at 12 noon promptly, and that any member not then in his place would forfeit his expenses of 10s 6d.

The meeting ordered that Hodgkinson should continue to mark out the line extending back to Fforddfawr and onward to Eardisley. It appears that little thought had been given to the manner of crossing the Wye at Whitney, and Hodgkinson was instructed to prepare plans and specifications for a bridge. Crosley's plans had shown the proposed crossing to be about 200 yards upstream of the toll-bridge; Hodgkinson's showed it as immediately adjacent to it.[28]

The first payment to Bailey & Wayne for plates was made on 6 December 1811, when they received £700 on account. A further payment on account was made to the Clydach Ironworks. The sub-committee reported to this meeting that 'Mr Hodgkins' [*sic*] did not consider it worth while starting work on the flat land to the south of Hay and consequently no steps had been taken to acquire land there. At their last meeting they had come to the conclusion 'that the progress of the

THE HAY RAILWAY.

THE COMMITTEE, anxious to adopt the best Line of Road, and not being satisfied with the one drawn by Mr. CROSSLEY, employed Mr. JOHN HODGKINSON, Engineer, to Survey the Country through which the Road is intended to pass, who made the following Report.

Copy of Mr. HODGKINSON's Report.

IN pursuance of the Instructions of the Committee, I have surveyed and taken Levels of the Country through which the Railway is intended to pass, and by the Line on which the Act of Parliament has been obtained, I find the Rises and Falls to be—

	Length.		Rise.	Fall.	
	Miles.	Furls.	Feet.	Feet.	
From the Canal at Brecon to the Summit of the Hill at Blaen Brynich	3	6	309	—	Being 12 inches in each 22 yards.
From Blaen Brynich to Tregunter	4	0	—	293	11 inches in each 22 yards.
From Tregunter to Glasbury	4	4	—	160	5½ inches in each 22 yards.
From Glasbury to Hay Bridge	4	0	—	50	2 inches in each 22 yards.
From Hay Bridge to Purton Cross	7	0	—	22	Half an inch in each 22 yards.
Total	23	2	309	525	

The disadvantages attendant on the Working of a Railway in which the Rise in the first instance is so steep, and the ensuing Falls are so unequally divided, will appear more forcibly from the Estimate of the Charges of Hauling thereon, hereafter stated. than by any other explanation I can give.

Having at the last Meeting submitted the propriety of altering the Line, by commencing at New Bridge, and taking the road through Llanvihangel Tallyllyn, and having received the directions of the Committee to take up the Line from the old point, at the Wharf at Brecon, and plan the best Road from thence, I have done so, and made Two Lines, the one through Keven North, by means of a short Tunnel, and the other round that Hill—I recommend to the Company the Line round the Hill, as the summit turns out to be 34 Feet lower than can be obtained by a short

2

unnel, and is more gradually attained.—To these reasons should be added a consi-
erable difference of Expense, as will appear by the Estimates.

The Rises and Falls on this Line I find to be:—

	Length.		Rise.		Fall.	
	Miles.	Furl.	Feet.	In.	Feet.	
rom the Canal at Brecon to the Summit of the Hill at Clygyfach	4	5	154	2		Being 5 inches in every 22 yards.
etween Llanvihangel and Llangorse Pool, on the left of Trewalter Farm, and to the right of Treveccs, through Talgarth and Great Porthamel Farm, to the Three Cocks, and thence on the upper side of Glasbury Church to Hay	14	0	—		348	Which may be divided into Two Falls of 5 inches to Glasbury, and 3 inches to Hay.
rom Hay to Eardisley, as in the Act of Parliament Line	7	3			22	Half an inch in each 22 yards.
Total	26	0	154	2	370	

I have also Planned some variations in the direction of the Line between Hay and
ardisley, which will be satisfactory to the Land Owners, and occasion a considerable
aving to the Company in the Purchase of Land, and in Fencing, without lengthening
r injuring the Road in any respect.

The Company will observe that by the Line I have proposed, the Hill which inter-
enes between Brecon and Hay is surmounted, at an Elevation of 154 Feet 2 Inches,
hich is about one half less than by the Act of Parliament Line.

That the fall to Hay being regular and moderate, much greater facility will be
Forded to the Back Carriage.

On the Act of Parliament Line, One Horse would only Haul One Ton either way,
ver the elevation of 309 Feet. On the proposed Amended Line, One Horse will be
ble to draw Three Tons each way, over the elevation of 154 Feet: and I estimate
ne Charges of Hauling on the Act of Parliament Line to be:—

	£.	s.	d.
From Brecon to Hay, per Ton of Coal	0	3	1
From Hay to Eardisley, per Ditto	0	0	8
	£.0	3	9

Back Carriage from Eardisley to Brecon, per Ton	0	4	0
Ditto, ... from Hay to Brecon	0	3	6

The Expense of making this Line of Road, including the Purchase of Land,
encing, and all other incidental Charges, I estimate at the Sum of £.57,603 18s. 6d.
I estimate the Charges of Hauling on the Line of Road last proposed, at—

	£.	s.	d.
From Brecon to Hay, per Ton of Coal	0	1	9
From Hay to Eardisley, per Ditto	0	0	8
	£.0	2	5

Back Carriage from Eardisley to Brecon, per Ton	0	1	9
Ditto, ... from Hay to Brecon	0	1	9

3

The Expense of making this Line of Road, including the Purchase of Land,
Fencing, and all other incidental Expenses, I estimate at the Sum of £.50,375 12s.

In addition to this saving in the Expense of making the Road and in the Charges
of Hauling, the Expense of keeping the last proposed Line in Repair will be less by
£.300 per Annum, than the Act of Parliament Line.

JOHN HODGKINSON.

Hay, September 30th, 1811.

━━━━━●❋●━━━━━

At a General Meeting of the Proprietors held this Day, the
above Report was taken into consideration, and Mr. HODGKIN-
SON having produced a Plan of his Line of Road, from the
Wharf of the Brecknock and Abergavenny Canal at Brecon,
round Keven North Hill, through Llanvihangel Tallyllyn, Talgarth, and Hay, to the Village of Eardisley; *It was Resolved* to
adopt this Line, and that the Committee should make application to Parliament the next Session to Amend the present Act,
and in the mean time proceed in making the Road on such
parts of the Line as the present Act will admit of.—Two
Thousand Tons of Tram Plates having been Contracted for, a
considerable part Delivered, and the remainder in a state of
forwardness for Delivery.

JAMES SPENCER,
Clerk to the Company.

Hay, September 30th, 1811.

8. The report presented to the
committee of the Hay Railway by
John Hodgkinson in September 1811
in which he recommended a route
around Cefn North Hill rather than
the Talyllyn tunnel through the hill.
By permission of Hereford and
Worcester County Libraries

work will be much promoted' by concentrating on 'the deep cutting between Sheep House and the river Dulas [SO 230427] and at Pontfane Dingle' (SO 234438) where a side-cut had to be made in the steep bank of the Wye. The committee ordered that land at those places should be purchased, and a further call of £10 per share, due on 6 January 1812, should be made.

An advertisement addressed to 'Quarry-men, Stone Cutters, Diggers, etc.' appeared in the *Hereford Journal* of 18 December 1811 asking for tenders for the supply of 20,000 stone blocks, each to be 6 inches thick, to weigh 68 pounds and to be bored to specification and delivered at Hay. Those interested were to attend the committee on 8 January 1812. The same meeting would be prepared to receive tenders from persons wishing to contract for preparing the line near Hay. Specifications of the work required in both cases would be available at Spencer's office in Hay on the previous day.

On 8 January 1812 the committee considered a letter from a Mr Parry who was concerned lest his orchard near Eardisley should be disturbed by the making of the tramroad. Spencer was instructed to reply that the committee would avoid his property. It is surprising that Parry had not raised the point before, as the plot is shown to have been in his occupation when the 1810 Act was passed and is shown in the schedule to the Act under No. 393. The plans for the Bill which was being sought in 1812 show the plot in the same occupation and liable to 'compulsory purchase' under 'Herefordshire No. 408'.

Considerable disquiet was expressed at this meeting at the number of people in arrears with their calls, and Spencer was instructed to write to all who fell into this category to inform them that a contract had been let for the formation of the tramroad near Hay and that arrangements had been made for the supply of plates for the whole line. Consequently the committee

… find themselves under the disagreeable necessity of ordering at the next meeting that the solicitor shall proceed against all such persons.

The contract to form the track-bed from 'the gate of Lord Hereford's field in Cusop towards the Sheephouse' was signed on 8 January 1812 with John Williams of Llanfoist and John Jones of Abergavenny in the sum of £1,400 for the mile to be made. The same parties contracted to deliver 20,000 stone blocks at 7½d each, sufficient for just over five miles of track.

On 20 January Thomas Bold advised Sir Charles Morgan that he had heard that a meeting in opposition to the company's new Bill was to be called, but that as yet he had little information.[29] Two days later an advertisement appeared in the *Hereford Journal* calling all shareholders

… who are anxious to adopt a shorter and better line of Road … and who intend to petition against the unnecessary expense of an amendment to the present Bill …

to meet at the *Swan Inn,* Hay on 13 February. On 29 January the paper carried another notice asking the shareholders to suspend judgment on the previous notice as

… they may rest assured that the Company of the Proprietors at their last General Meeting did not decide on the plan submitted to them without due deliberation …

and that the committee must be accountable to the general meeting and not to a meeting irregularly convened 'for the purpose of forwarding a plan which can never be brought within the scope of their Act of Parliament'. Another notice in the paper of 12 February stated that thirty-two of those who had signed a petition against the new Act had changed their minds, and urged all who could to attend a general meeting to be held that day, 'when a plan of the improved line will be submitted for their inspection'. On 15 February Spencer was instructed to proceed with the Bill which he had drafted, as no other plan had been submitted to the committee.

In spite of the existence of discontent the Bill received its first reading in the Commons on 27 January, and was read a second time and committed on 4 February.[30] With the Bill in Committee, the meetings of the Hay committee were moved to London to be on hand to give evidence.

The *Hereford Journal* of 26 February reported that Thomas Harcourt Powell of Peterstone Court (SO 088265) had lodged a petition against the Bill, and *The Cambrian* of 14 March stated that George Overton had done likewise. A third petition by the Rev. Thomas Watkins on the grounds that he did not approve of the new route, and asking that his name might be withdrawn from the list of subscribers and that the money which he had paid should be re-imbursed was rejected out of hand at a meeting of the committee held at the *Cannon Coffee House,* Charing Cross on 3 March. Overton had given the same reason for his petition,[31] but in view of later happenings he may well have had other motives.

Powell's petition was on very different grounds. Despite the Parliamentary notice of the intention to construct Hodgkinson's 'tunnel line', the general meeting of 30 September 1811 had decided to apply, in the Bill, for the line around Cefn North Hill, the route preferred by Hodgkinson. It appears that Powell and his cousin, the Rev. Thomas Powell, Rector of Llanhamlach, had examined the plans and schedule in the offices of the Clerk of the Peace in Brecon and had found that the parish of Llansantffraed, through which the now approved line passed for a short distance, had been omitted from the schedule, although it was mentioned in the press notice. A month after the cousins had examined the plans and schedule a chance meeting with the Clerk of the Peace had led them to take another look, when they found that the parish concerned had been inserted at the end of the schedule. Both gentlemen were certain that it had not previously been there. Powell considered that the attention of the House should be drawn to this irregularity, and stated that both he and his cousin would be prepared to give evidence that the formalities had not been complied with. He cited a number of other points: the line as now proposed would lead through a part of his estate already intersected by the canal and several turnpikes, and the articles that it was proposed to carry, coal and lime, could more easily be distributed to his lands directly by canal. He considered the proposed line of the tramroad to be 'an act of wanton oppression'. Should the tramroad terminate at Brynich competition would be stimulated, but making all goods go first to Brecon tended 'strongly to monopoly'.[32] On 3 March 1812 the committee resolved that Sir Charles Morgan and Thomas Wood, both Members of Parliament and on the Hay committee, should confer with Powell

at the Temple in an endeavour to induce him to withdraw his petition.

From his petition it is obvious that Powell considered that the tramroad should terminate at the canal at Brynich. Morgan confirmed that this was also his opinion in a Memorandum of Agreement, signed by him and the Hay committee on 4 March 1812, by which he undertook to let the tramroad company have land for such a line, reserving to himself the right to construct a wharf and erect a crane.[33]

The committee met at Morgan's house in Pall Mall on 7 March, when he reported that Powell had agreed with him and Wood that the company should abandon the line around the hill and press on with the tunnel line. Powell was to be allowed £200 towards his expenses in altering the line of the Llanvihangel turnpike and he agreed to sell to the company any land needed to make the connecting line to the canal at Brynich.

Two days later the committee decided that to construct a branch to Brynich after the main line had been completed would satisfy a number of the petitioners, and resolved that even if it proved impossible to include it in the Bill it should be made by private treaty. To do so would be easy, as the only two landowners concerned were in favour. The meeting concluded by ordering a payment of £50 to Hodgkinson with which to pay the contractors for the work in progress near Hay: Hodgkinson stated that this was insufficient, and Spencer was accordingly instructed to pay him £150.

Writing to Morgan on 11 March, Hugh Bold expressed surprise that it had been decided to make the branch at all, a decision of which he had been informed by both Spencer and Wood. On receiving the information he had spoken to a number of people, all of whom had expressed a 'considerable degree of alarm'. Those whom he mentioned by name were all connected with the canal company! His letter continued:

… it is very obvious what the intention of the proposed clause is and *to me,* equally so who is the *Father of it.* If there is any power given to the Hay rail-way Co. to communicate with the canal at Newbridge it is quite clear that the coal will be carried along that Road by a channel other than the canal … As being the person on the part of the Canal Company who was deputed to signify their sanction to the Hay Rail-way passing through their lands … I feel myself imperiously called upon to acquaint them with this alteration … and shall attend tomorrow.[34]

Bold's 'Father of it' is probably a reference to George Overton, who at the time was planning the Brinore Tramroad, and envisaged a possible tramroad connection from Talybont on Usk to Talyllyn.

When the canal committee met on 12 March Hugh Bold notified them that he had signed the agreement for the Hay Railway to use canal lands at Brecon, and he then reported the latest decision of the tramroad company of which he had been advised by his correspondents. The canal committee immediately passed a resolution that the branch would be prejudicial to their interests and that measures should be taken to register opposition in the House by sending the company's solicitors, Powell & Jones of Brecon, to London.[35]

Thomas Bold advised Morgan of the B&A's decision on 14 March, and reported that he had been asked to sign a petition against the suggested branch, which he understood had been organised by Edward Frere of the Clydach Ironworks, but had declined to do so.[36]

The Hay committee met in the office of the Commons on 16 March, and without transacting any business immediately adjourned the meeting to the *Glosster* [*sic*] *Coffee House* in Piccadilly. There they received a deputation from the B&A who informed them of the canal company's official view, and demanded that the Hay Bill in its original form should be prosecuted in both Houses. The Hay committee passed a resolution that the Bill

… as amended by the Committee of the House of Commons and transmitted to Hugh Bold Esquire for the information of the canal company should, without any additional clause or alteration, be prosecuted in both Houses of Parliament. That no application be made to enlarge, alter or diminish the power contained therein.

Spencer was instructed to notify the B&A officially of the decision.

The B&A deputation attended the Hay committee again at the same place on 18 March, when Jones, the B&A solicitor, produced a petition signed by several freeholders of Brecon praying that a clause might be introduced into the Bill

… prohibiting the Hay Rail-way Company from taking any advantage of the clause in the Brecknock & Abergavenny Canal Act authorising the making of collateral branches to the said canal.

The clause referred to was the 'eight mile clause'. This was the petition which Thomas Bold refused to sign.

Demonstrating the rapidity with which the Post Office could perform its function in 1812, when the Hay committee again met at the coffee house on 20 March, Jones was ready for them with a copy of a resolution passed by the B&A committee on 18 March stating that

… this committee would very imperfectly execute the trust reposed in them by the Company of Proprietors of this Canal Navigation if they suffered the intended Rail-way Bill to pass into a law in its present shape without giving it their decided opposition.

At the same time they declare they are ready to give every facility to the passing of the said intended Bill with such modifications as may not in any wise interfere with or prejudice the interests of this concern.

Those members of their committee who were then in London were authorised to conclude any agreement that might be to the mutual advantage of the two concerns.

It seems finally to have been understood by the Hay committee at this meeting that the B&A was worried lest the Hay Railway should invoke the eight mile clause to construct the branch to Brynich at some time in the future. The committee passed a resolution disclaiming any such intention and stating that they were under the impression that the clause could only apply to owners of lands containing mines or minerals. They had considered that the B&A would be amply protected by the clause in their intended Bill which limited deviations to 100 yards from the planned line. In its final phrases the resolution concluded:

The members of the committee now present distinctly avow they as a Company have no idea or conception of ever making any work connecting with the Canal other than the line in the Plan and the communication to Newbridge.[37]

There seems to have been no further opposition from the B&A and the Bill went through its final stages in the Commons on 20 March, and with no amendments arising in the Lords it received the Royal Assent on 20 May 1812.[38]

CHAPTER THREE

THE HAY RAILWAY
Completion to Hay
(1812 – 1816)

WHILE the committee had been meeting in London some progress had been made at home. On 13 April 1812 Hodgkinson certified that Williams and Jones had completed work to the value of £430 on their contract near Hay; but in a cautious vein (or perhaps with an eye to the state of the finances) the committee authorised a payment to them of £200 only. Bailey & Wayne had delivered more plates and were paid £500 on account, and Spencer was allowed to draw £60 for costs he had met for 'haling' (i.e. hauling) plates delivered at Talgarth to the line of the tramroad at Hay.

The committee minutes for 4 May 1812 are headed – in pencil – that it was the first meeting 'after the passing of the Act for the amending of the line of Railway'. Royal Assent was not given until 20 May and it can only be assumed that the pencil note referred to the date of the third reading in the Lords.

Hodgkinson was instructed by the meeting to mark out the ground from Brecon to Hay and to divide the line shown on the plans into three sections; the first from Brecon to near Trewalter (SO 128297), the second from this point to Porthamel (SO 157353), and the third from Porthamel to where Williams & Jones were working near Sheephouse (SO 211415). Spencer was ordered to advertise in the papers that the committee would consider tenders at its meeting on 19 June and that contracts would be awarded to the lowest bidders. He was also to advertise for 'plans and proposals for building a wooden bridge over the Wye adjacent to the existing bridge'. Frere & Co. were paid another £500 on account, and Hodgkinson received his fee of £100 for surveying. Spencer was instructed to write again to those in arrears of their calls.

The advertisement did not appear in the *Hereford Journal* until 10 June, nor until 20 June in *The Cambrian*, by which time the wording decided on in May had been amended by a meeting on 1 June to include the fact that one of the contracts would include making a tunnel for 600 yards through Cefn North Hill. The part of the advertisement referring to the bridge now stated more specifically that it was to be 'an OAK TIMBER BRIDGE on Piles … (the roadway thereof to be nine feet wide)'. The deadline for receiving tenders was extended to 3 July, and it was stated that the ground would be marked out by 27 June, on which date the plans would be available for inspection.

On 2 June Spencer advised Sir Charles Morgan that

By the Hay Railway Treasurer's Book you stand in arrears for the last call of 10% due 6th. January, which it would be pleasant to have paid within the month of June.

He continued:

I am writing to every subscriber in arrears of which there seem a great many & hope to get most of the money in before the next meeting which is fixed for 3rd. July. Mr. Watkins of Donoyre has only paid £50 in part of these calls amounting to £300.[39]

9. The site of the Watton wharf at Brecon, the starting point of the Hay Railway. The tramroad ran on the northern (left) bank of the Brecknock & Abergavenny Canal, passing under the arch which is partially obscured by vegetation. The wharf itself has been covered by landfill at a later date to provide a storage area for an adjacent garage. Photo: C. R. Clinker collection, Brunel University Library (*c*.1960)

At the meeting Spencer was again instructed to write to all those who were in arrears, and to point out that unless money was forthcoming it would be impossible to continue construction. Perhaps a little optimistically, a fourth call was made of £10 per share due on 3 August.

A number of payments were made at the meeting of 3 July. Bailey & Wayne received £300 and Frere & Co. £500 for tramplates; Williams & Jones £300 on account of their contract; Spencer £300 on account of his bill and his salary of £200 per annum; Hodgkinson another £200; and James Price £7 8s 6d 'for the scale and weights bought for weighing the iron'. The Treasurer, William Williams, had died and John Parry Wilkins of Wilkins' Bank was appointed to act until the next general meeting.

Several construction contracts were let on 3 July. The contract from the Watton wharf was awarded to Robert Tipping who undertook to make the line from there to 'a road crossing the road from Llanvihangel Talyllyn to Llangorse' (SO 117284) for £7,550 including the tunnel. The minutes describe Tipping as 'a miner of Newnham, Gloucester', but there is little doubt that he had been the contractor for the Haie tunnel on the Bullo Pill Railway in the Forest of Dean. Hodgkinson had been the engineer of this line,[40] the tunnel being completed by September 1809.[41] He had also been the contractor for the abortive tunnel

under the Severn from near Newnham to Arlingham on the southern bank of the river. This venture had failed when the river broke into the workings on 13 November 1812 when it was half way under the river.[42] He had sub-contracted under Hodgkinson when the latter built the new bridge over the Usk at Caerleon in 1805.[43] No doubt the Hay committee considered themselves fortunate to obtain the services of so experienced a contractor, and one who was known to their engineer.

The section from the end of Tipping's contract to Porthamel and on to join the work of Williams & Jones at Sheephouse was let in two lots to Anthony Tissington and John Thacker at £3,750 for each lot. Nothing is known of the antecedents of these two gentlemen, and it is possible, in view of the times and the lack of railway contracting experience, that they were local labourers who saw the possibility of making some money.

On 3 August 1812 Spencer was instructed to contact all who were in default on calls: those who were three calls in arrears were to be warned of possible prosecution, while those who were two calls adrift were to be given until the next meeting on 31 August to pay. The meeting authorised a payment of £600 to Frere & Co. for plates and £200 to Williams & Jones 'on account of further work done and for blocks', but the minutes do not specify how much was due for each item.

10. Bridge over the B&A Canal and the Hay Railway at Brecon (opposite face to that shown in FIG.9). The tramroad passed through the far arch to reach its terminus at the Watton wharf which lay just on the other side of the bridge. Photo: C. R. Clinker collection, Brunel University Library (*c.*1960)

How serious the position was in respect of calls is revealed in a letter of 1 July from Thomas Bold to Sir Charles Morgan informing him that he had paid £250 each in respect of calls due for the Rev. Thomas Watkins, Sir Charles himself and his son, and informing him of the possibility of the company taking legal action against defaulters, of whom there were a considerable number.[44]

Meeting on 31 August 1812 the committee confirmed payment of Spencer's salary at £200 per annum as from the previous September, and allowed him his bills for £1,582 9s 7d and £981 10s 10d in respect of the company's two Acts. It is not known if these amounts were in addition to the payments of £1,000 and £300 already made on this account. Spencer reported that, to date, he had taken no action in respect of arrears of calls and was instructed to do so immediately. Williams & Jones were paid another £180, and, on Hodgkinson's certificates, Tissington & Thacker were paid £200 and Tipping £150. David Davies, the surveyor for Breconshire, was paid £100 on account.

Committee meetings were apparently somewhat convivial affairs, and this led to the passing of the following resolution on 31 August:

… that the wine ordered by James Jones Esquire at the request of several gentlemen of the Committee amounting to £76 6s be paid for by the Treasurer of this Company to Mr. John Blannin, and that the same be re-imbursed by the several Members of the Committee who have partaken or shall hereafter partake of the same out of their allowance of Ten shillings and Six pence.

The identity of Mr Blannin is not known; he was not the landlord of the *Swan Inn*, for the next entry in the minutes recorded a payment of £13 13s to Joseph Ward, *Swan Inn*, 'for expences of the Committee to date'.

An advertisement by the company in the *Hereford Journal* of 9 September 1812 addressed to 'Railway Makers, Diggers, &c.' called for tenders 'for forming and finishing a part of the said Railway at the termination of the Road near Hay, to a meadow below Bontfaen known as Muck Mill Meadow' (SO 234437 approx.), a length of about one mile. Ten days later the contract was awarded to Peter Murphy, yeoman of Abergavenny, in the sum of £646. Murphy had been one of the contractors for extending the B&A Canal from Llanfoist to Pontymoile, and had borrowed money from the canal company to enable him to make a tramroad to carry the materials necessary.[45] At a time when experienced tramroad contractors were hard to find, even such a slight acquaintance with the requirements was probably considered a recommendation.

A number of payments for land were made at the committee meeting on 19 September. In

11. Afon Llynfi bridge. The Hay Railway ran on an embankment built on top of the bridge. Construction began in 1812 with Tissington & Thacker as the contractors. When they failed to make satisfactory progress the contract was transferred to Peter Murphy in 1813. Photo: P. G. Rattenbury (1975)

several cases the company had to pay extra for growing timber to a total of about £1,000. There was a further payment of £500 for tramplates to Frere & Co. Spencer was paid £460

… on further account of business done by him and money paid by him on account of the Railway, and for his salary as Clerk to the Company.

After paying £120 to Tipping and £200 to Tissington & Thacker it cannot have been a surprise that it was decided to call another £10 per share, due on 19 October 1812.

The weather appears to have been fine during the autumn of 1812 and the contractors were able to get on with their work in earnest; by 24 November Williams & Jones drew £280, Tipping £800 and Tissington & Thacker £950. Tissington & Thacker appear to have been under-capitalised, and the large amount of work which they had undertaken was stretching their resources somewhat. The meeting therefore authorised Spencer to draw £400 to be advanced to them on their giving suitable security. These payments, together with a further £560 paid for land, necessitated another call of £10 per share due on 25 December.

Advances of £300 each were made to Tissington & Thacker in both December 1812 and January 1813, and in February Spencer was authorised to draw another £800 to be passed to them on the same conditions as the advance in November 1812. It is doubtful if they received this last amount as on 9 March Hodgkinson reported that they 'were not proceeding with their work with sufficient speed agreeable to the terms of their contract with the Company'. The contract was declared void and Hodgkinson was authorised to find other contractors.

The skirmish with the Hay Railway while their Act was before Parliament had alerted the B&A to the possible dangers to their trade that might arise from their eight-mile clause. On 26 June 1812 the B&A committee was attended by only three members, two of whom, Edward Frere and Hugh Bold, were both also on the tramroad committee, but favoured the prosperity of the canal rather than that of the tramroad company. The canal committee decided that the time had come to apply to Parliament to have the clause rescinded. Additional point was given to their arguments on

12. A train emerges from the western portal of Talyllyn tunnel, as it might have appeared during the existence of the Hay Railway. Tie bars, or iron sleepers, were used in the tunnel where it was particularly important to ensure that the track was kept to gauge.
Drawing: Edward Paget-Tomlinson

13 October when Benjamin Hall of Rhymney Ironworks applied for a tramroad from his works to Talybont on Usk, by which coal from the Rhymney valley intended for Brecon could be shipped on the canal at a point 11½ miles nearer to that town than the shipping point of the Brecknock Boat Company at Gilwern. A special general meeting of canal shareholders on 11 December confirmed the committee's views, and on the following day Hugh Bold notified Sir Charles Morgan of the outcome of the meeting.[46] On 19 January 1813 the question was discussed thoroughly at the Hay committee meeting when it was resolved that it was of such importance that it was

proposed to call a general meeting to consider opposition to the canal company's proposal. In the event the B&A's bill was rejected in the Commons on a motion by Sir Charles on 5 March 1813, and the way was clear for what later became the Brinore Tramroad to Talybont on Usk.[47]

At the time that the Hay Railway was under construction John Hodgkinson was a very busy man, being engineer to both the Llanvihangel and the Grosmont Railways (both plateways) whose plans were also taking shape. It was not until 22 December 1812 that the minute book makes clear what his position was with the Hay Railway with a resolution that …

13. Former trackbed of the Hay Railway north of the Llynfi embankment.
The tramroad crossed the road from Llanfihangel Talyllyn to Trefeinon and ran between the lines of trees.
The trees have now been uprooted and the trackbed can barely be discerned. This formed part of the section
commenced by Tissington & Thacker in 1812 and transferred to Peter Murphy in 1813.
Photo: P. G. Rattenbury (1968)

… the Treasurer do pay John Hodgkinson and William Dunsford the sum of £200 on account of their contract for superintending the works of this concern.

No record has been seen of their appointment but this must have been made at a general meeting for which the minute book is no longer available. C. R. Clinker quotes Dunsford's name as William B. Dunsford.[48] Probably he is the same man who was Agent to the Bullo Pill Company in 1810 at the time that Hodgkinson was their engineer.[49]

Tissington & Thacker were not the only contractors who lacked adequate experience. On 19 January 1813 Spencer was instructed to 'take measures' against Williams & Jones for non-fulfilment of their contract. He was also to call on them to recompense the landowners in respect of stone that had been removed from their lands and sold. They were paid £30 on account with a further payment of £80 on 25 May, after which they disappear from the record. In all Williams & Jones were paid £1,870, but it is not known what proportion of this represents payment for the supply of blocks. Only two payments to them are shown as being on account of their contract and of their supplying blocks.

On 23 February 1813 the company made a seventh call of £10 per share due on 29 March, and on 15 March Tissington & Thacker's two contracts were re-allocated in five lots. The first two, from Llangorse Lane (SO 122283) to Pont Nichol Lane (SO 144330) were taken by Peter Murphy in the sum of £2,906; the remaining three lots, from Pont Nichol Lane to connect with Williams & Jones near Sheephouse, were allocated to John and Hugh Allen for £5,770. The whole length had originally carried a price of £7,500, and now, after some work had been done and paid for, mainly between Llangorse Lane and Pont Nichol, the cost was likely to be a further £8,676 – a fair indication of the lack of experience of the contractors! The surveyor, David Davies, was instructed to attend the next meeting with details of the work required from each contractor.

It was reported to the meeting on 15 March that Tissington & Thacker had completed sufficient work to cover the advance of £400 made in November 1812, and their sureties were released from their bond. As previously stated, it is unlikely that £800 paid to Spencer on 23 February 1813 to advance to them had been paid over.

To judge by the size of the payments made to the contractors in 1813, the weather throughout the year must have been exceptionally favourable. From February to October payments totalled to Tipping £3,900, to Murphy £2,317, and to the Allens £3,320. In the same period the following year Tipping was paid only £950 and the other two surrendered their contracts.

Another call of £10 per share was made by the committee on 25 May 1813, due on 25 June, but the non-payment of previous calls was still a cause for concern and Spencer was instructed to report to all subsequent meetings the names of those against whom he had instituted proceedings. On 6 July, in order to instil a greater promptitude into the shareholders, he was instructed to write to all in arrears stating that

… the rapidity with which the works are now going on and the necessity of continuing every exertion at this favourable season of the year occasions very heavy demands on the Company's funds. That the Committee is already considerably indebted to the Treasurer and that therefore an immediate payment of all arrears is absolutely necessary for the effectual prosecution of the works and the prosperity of the concern.

There appears to have been little response to the letters and on 19 July it was resolved to write again to those who had not replied, and at the Decem-

14. Partially buried archway through an embankment near Trefeca (SO 138317), also on the section initially assigned to Tissington & Thacker and completed by Peter Murphy. It is not certain whether it was a cattle creep or a footway, but it is probably the only surviving Hay Railway bridge or culvert that is not over water. Photo: Tim Edmonds (1992)

ber committee meeting it was suggested that a special general meeting should be called to declare void all unpaid shares.

Anxious to keep expenditure down, on 10 August the committee decided that 'there is more than sufficient iron [i.e. tramplates] for the immediate purposes of Hay Railway', and it was resolved to terminate the contract with Bailey & Wayne and to pay them the balance of their account by two bills of exchange, one for £439 10s 3d at three months and one of £305 6s 3d at six months. The ironmasters protested and in February 1814 the chairman, Viscount Hereford, was asked to write assuring them that they would be allowed interest on the outstanding amounts.

The final call of £10 per share due on 18 March 1814 was made on 15 February, when it was again suggested that a special general meeting should be held to declare void all shares with outstanding balances. The special meeting was held on 16 March at which it was decided that if the shares were forfeited the company would lose the possibility of ever obtaining the full value unless someone could be found to take up the partly paid shares. It was thought that a more satisfactory procedure would be to sue the offenders in the courts. On 22 March Spencer, in his capacity as Clerk, was instructed to notify those concerned of the decision of the meeting.

Hodgkinson reported on 13 May that John and Hugh Allen had 'withdrawn themselves and their workmen from the line of Road contracted for by them', and was instructed to take the necessary steps to get possession of the works and to employ men to ensure that the fences and gates, at least, were all made, and to make enquiries for competent persons to take over the contract, in particular someone to complete the bridges, and to report to the next meeting.

Hodgkinson did not attend the meeting on 24 May 1814 and it was ordered that a letter should be sent to him stating that the committee 'have been much dis-appointed by his non-attendance'. Dunsford, who was present, was instructed to obtain the services of a person competent to make bridges over the river 'Eigon' (i.e. Enig) at Talgarth (SO 153339) and the brook in Gwernyfed Park (SO 170373).

Another blow fell on 16 August when it was learnt that Peter Murphy had withdrawn his men, and Spencer was instructed to obtain possession of the work. The committee, wearied by the unreliability of contractors, ordered that in their next monthly report to them the joint engineers should

… set forth particularly the sum of money that will be required to finish the Road to Hay and what sum will be required to make and complete the Road to a convenient spot for a wharf near Whitney Bridge …

evidently intending to dispense with contractors and complete the line by direct labour.

Whilst the Hay Railway had been passing through a series of crises to semi-completion, Hodgkinson had completed the Llanvihangel Railway (a plateway) from Govilon to Blaengavenny and was actively engaged on its extension to Llanvihangel Crucorney and Llangua.[50] No mention has been found of his being granted leave of absence from the Hay Railway and, probably after discussing his frequent lack of attendance, the Hay committee voted on 18 September 1814 to pay Hodgkinson and Dunsford their joint quarter's salary of £200 and ordered that

… Mr William Dunsford be and he is hereby appointed Resident Engineer of the Works at a salary after the rate of £400 per annum.

Hodgkinson is not mentioned in the minutes for the next ten months.

Williams & Jones appear to have had scant regard for the properties through which their construction contract took them, and on 22 March 1815, on Dunsford's recommendation, the committee ordered that £30 should be paid to Thomas James 'for the stone and other materials taken by the tramroad contractor and for damages committed to his property' in view of the fact that James had undertaken to make and maintain the tramroad fences where the line passed through his land.

The minutes of this meeting reveal the company's poor financial position. This is apparent in the order given that Spencer should write to the partners in the Brecon Bank requesting

… that they will advance the Hay Railway £2,500 to enable the Committee to carry on the works of the Railway on the security of two gentlemen members hereof.

The minutes do not record the bank's reply, but an entry on 15 December 1817 possibly refers to this transaction with the bankers, when the committee were informed that the Treasurer, John Parry Wilkins (one of the partners in the bank), had expressed his willingness to accept the company's note for £2,100 in part payment of their indebtedness to him. Spencer was instructed to issue a promissory note for the amount, payable at seven years from the following Christmas with interest to be paid annually. There is no proof that

15. Bridge carrying the Hay Railway over the river Enig at Talgarth.
Photo: R. A. Cook (1960)

the two items were related but it would appear highly likely.[51]

It had already been foreseen that a shortage of money was likely to be a problem, and on 21 April 1815 the committee decided to give effect to a general meeting resolution of the previous September to raise money by means of the 'Hay Railway Optional Loan'. The committee laid down that the loan should be a charge on the assets of the company; that interest should be payable at 5 per cent per annum; that promissory notes should be issued for amounts borrowed, repayable on six months notice being given in the *London Gazette;* and that at any time within the first five years of the loan's currency holders should have the option of converting their notes into £100 shares in the company. At the com-

mittee meeting on 21 April loans totalling £330 were immediately offered plus an unspecified sum from Sir Charles Morgan. By December 1816 £6,805 had been received on this account.[52]

Dunsford reported to the committee on 21 July that Robert Tipping had found that he would not be able to complete his part of the contracted line for £7,750, and the committee deemed it 'prudent to enter into a new contract with him to finish the work at an advanced sum of £970'. The exact amount of the additional contract is unknown, as there is a marginal note in the minute book stating that 'The sum ought to be £935'. Hodgkinson's name re-appeared in the minutes of this meeting in the role of a contractor: he had undertaken to finish the line from the end of Tipping's contract to The Lakes (Lakes Cottage)

33

(SO 251465) for £3,500 to include the fencing, the company to pay for the land and the actual track.

Hodgkinson had completed work to the value of £400 by 18 August when the committee revised the terms of his contract to £2,975 for completing the track formation exclusive of fencing, plus £15 per annum per mile to keep it in repair for ten years. Fences were the subject of a separate contract under which he was to be paid £525 to make them from Brecon to Whitney, plus £15 per annum per mile to keep them in order for the next five years, followed by another five years at £15 per annum per mile, adding somewhat unnecessarily that the tunnel was not included in the mileage to be fenced!

It is not known how Hodgkinson's second contract was affected by arrangements entered into by Thomas Rowbridge, who was to be paid £20 for fences to be made by him at Ffordffawr (SO 191397) and by T. Y. Wheeler of Sheephouse Farm who was to be paid £30 to make the fences through the farm provided that his tenant, a Mr Trownsir, would undertake that no cost should fall on the company until the quicksets should have matured.

James Spencer was by no means a poor man, which was perhaps fortunate for the tramroad company on occasions, but his habit of making payments on their behalf without consulting the committee must, at times, have been embarrassing.

16. Llanfihangel Talyllyn embankment, looking north-east.
The white-walled house is Arrah Lodge, built across the tramroad at a later date. Thomas Ellwood, the mineral agent of the Brecknock Boat Co., noted in 1816 that this and other embankments were, in his opinion, too narrow and liable to slippage.
Photo: Stephen K. Jones (1994)

17. A train of waggons crosses Llanfihangel Talyllyn embankment.
They are loaded with coal, brought up the B&A Canal to Brecon and intended for sale in Hay or thereabouts.
Drawing: Edward Paget-Tomlinson

At the committee meeting on 21 November 1815 he was refunded £2,200 that he had paid to contractors from his own pocket. He appears to have governed every phase of the company's activities, and if he ever produced any accounts for the scrutiny of the committee there is no mention of them in the minutes. Possibly he produced figures for general meetings but this cannot be verified in the absence of the proprietors' minute book.

At the committee meeting on 19 March 1816 it came to light that only two of the promissory notes to be issued in return for loans under the Optional Loan scheme had been sealed by Spencer with the company's seal. He was instructed to rectify his omissions, dating all notes to 25 March 1816, and to ensure that interest was paid to all those who had subscribed from the date on which the money had actually been received.[53]

The tramroad appears to have been opened piecemeal. Confirmation of this is contained in a letter from Thomas Ellwood, the mineral agent and general factotum of the BBCo., which he wrote to his employers after he had inspected the line with a view to assessing its usefulness to his company. He considered that the section from Brecon to the middle of the tunnel, three and a half miles, would tax the strength of a good horse, but onwards to Hay the same horse would manage four tons despite an 'unregular' fall. He thought the embankments to be too narrow, and that being composed of a mixture of clay and sand, they would be apt to slip in wet weather until they had settled fully, which he judged would take two years. Little thought seemed to have been given to the location of possible wharves, a point that Ellwood considered should be settled, as otherwise owners of small parcels of land adjoining the tramroad might exercise their right under the Act to open wharves, in which case there was the possibility of more than was necessary being provided. At Hay, where the tramroad ran at a much lower level than the town, he thought that a site adjacent to the *Swan Inn* would be most suitable. He noted that the inn had recently been purchased by Sir Charles Morgan, possibly with the intention of opening a wharf there with the attendant pecuniary advantages, but he did not stress the latter point. He agreed that a wharf should be established at Glasbury as the bridge there would enable the tramroad to serve both sides of the river, but to have one at both Three Cocks and Talgarth would lead to difficulty in paying

… so many idle Agents as must be employed to look after them. I think I can venter in using the epithet idle for there must be a great change in times if they have much to do.

On 14 March Ellwood had observed two carts being loaded at Three Cocks with Brinore coal by the Agent and a labourer; it had been sold at 21s per ton. He had come to the conclusion that there was a good market for coal in the district served by the tramroad but he was uncertain how much the BBCO. could take. He thought that his company's

best course would be to wait to see how the trade developed. He suggested that the company should make a number of trams to be hired out to traders using the tramroad and purchasing their coal from the BBCO. Strict conditions should be imposed in respect of maintenance. Should a satisfactory trade develop the company would then be in a position to enter it on their own account. He thought that none of the BBCO's trams should be allowed onto the tramroad until the earthworks had settled in order to avoid any possible damage in use. Finally, he suggested that it might be possible, some time in the future, to send coal by boat from Hay to Hereford.[54]

Dunsford reported to the committee on 7 May 1816 that 'the Road of the Company is open and passable for all Persons from the Public Wharf at Brecon to the Bridge in the Town of Hay'. The committee proceeded to decide on the charges to be imposed for passage on the tramroad. These are detailed in TABLE A.

It must be remembered that the Hay Railway was not itself a carrier and its charges were solely for the use of the track, the owner or hirer of waggons being responsible for providing the means of haulage and hauliers to take charge of the waggons. It will be noted that the charges

TABLE A: Charges per ton/mile, 1811 and 1816.

Charges per ton/mile	AUTHORISED BY ACT OF 1811 [55]	COMMITTEE, 7 MAY 1816
Limestone, stone for road repair, dung, compost and manure (except lime)	2d	1½d
Lime, marl, sand, clay, peat, ironstone and other minerals, building stone, paving stone, bricks, tiles and slates	4d	2d
Coal, coke, stone coal, culm and cinders	4d	3d
Timber, pig or sheet lead, bar iron, wagon tires and all gross un-manufactured articles, building materials and grain	4d	4d
All other goods, commodities, wares and merchandizes	6d	6d

18. Culvert under the Llanfihangel Talyllyn embankment.
Photo: Stephen K. Jones (1994)

which the committee decided on were, in general, lower than those authorised by the Act, doubtless in an endeavour to stimulate trade.

The meeting instructed Dunsford to prepare 'a system of regulations for the Government of Persons and Carriages passing along, loading and unloading, upon the said Road', which was to be presented to the next meeting. He was also to arrange for a weighing machine, large enough to weigh two waggons, to be erected near the Llanvihangel turnpike, to erect a toll-house there, and to put down milestones as directed by the Act.

Richard Oliver was appointed as 'Agent and Clerk to the Company' at a salary of £70 per annum to commence 'as from the day he shall be required to enter into a Bond of Service'. His stipulated duties were 'to weigh Waggons, keep accounts, receive tonnages, and to be generally useful'. Finally the committee called a special general meeting of the proprietors to confirm their decisions and to decide on the erection of wharves.[56]

The *Hereford Journal* of 22 May 1816 reported that 'Yesterday se'enight [i.e. 14 May] the Tramroad from Brecon to Hay was finished and several waggons with coal arrived at the latter place'. The junketings usual on such occasions appear to have taken place, and the same issue of the paper reported the death of a labourer on the tramroad 'of a fever brought on by excessive drinking'.[57]

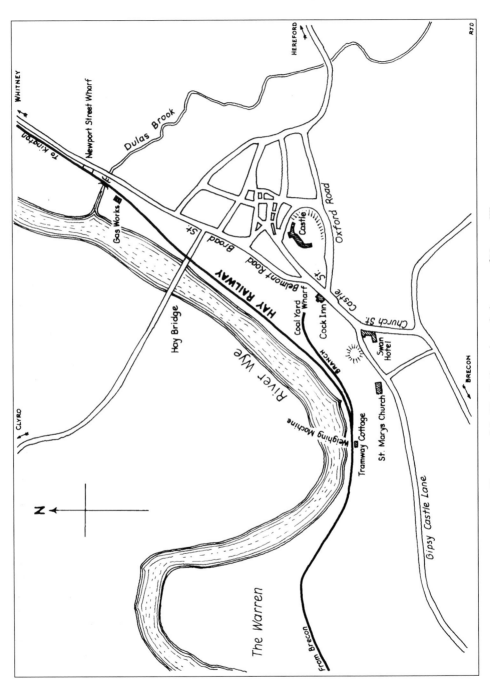

19. The route of the Hay Railway through the town of Hay-on-Wye.
Map: R. J. Dean

CHAPTER FOUR

THE HAY RAILWAY
Extension to Eardisley
(1816 – 1818)

THE tramroad officially opened for business on 14 May 1816, but it was not until a week before the opening that orders were given for the provision of a weighing-machine or a machine-house, neither of which could possibly have been provided in time. The B&A had more foresight and on 25 April they ordered

… a small machine to be erected on the Tram-Way in the wharf at the Watton, Brecon for taking account of the Canal limestone etc. passing along the Hay Railway at an expence not exceeding £21.[58]

This possibly reinforces Ellwood's evidence that the tramroad was opened piecemeal.[59] It is not known how tonnages were assessed at the commencement of trading – was reliance placed on the B&A's machine, or were the statements of the traders accepted as being accurate?

An advertisement in the *Hereford Journal* of 19 June 1816, offering coal for sale at Glasbury wharf, makes it obvious that the Brecknock Boat Company were the wholesalers. At Brecon the BBCO. had their own wharf on the canal at *The Cock & Horse* (SO 04752386) whereas the Hay Railway terminated at the Watton, about 500 yards to the east. The BBCO. had either to land their coal at the B&A's wharf at the Watton and pay wharfage or take it to their own wharf and pay cartage to take it to the Watton.

On 19 July the BBCO. and Hugh Bold, who had a wharf further west on the terminal arm of the canal (SO 04622835), jointly asked the B&A for a tramroad to be made under the canal Act from the Watton to the terminal. They would advance the money for this work which would be repaid by the B&A. On completion of the line they would jointly rent the tramroad at 5 per cent per annum of the actual cost. The B&A agreed and additionally sanctioned a tramroad from the canalside round their basin to connect with the Hay Railway.[60] It is surprising that the latter line had not been considered while the railway was under construction.

In order to stimulate trade in a downward direction, the committee decided on 23 July 1816 to allow a rebate of 1d per ton per mile on all 'Malt, Meal, Flour and Grain conveyed along this Railway'. Oliver's duties presumably commenced on the opening of the tramroad, for the same meeting ordered that all tonnages should be paid to Spencer at the Hay toll-bar or to Oliver at Llanhamlach as the loads passed. Should traders ask for credit they were to be required to sign a bond and to provide sureties for due payment. In these cases Oliver was to make up their accounts to the last Saturday in each month, and they were to be settled by bills of exchange at not more than sixty days either on London or on Wilkins' Bank, Brecon. Coal for lime burning, on which the tonnages were subject to a drawback, or rebate, of ½d per ton per mile, was an exception because it was a seasonal trade in which stocks were accumulated for the first six months of the year to ensure fresh supplies in the autumn. In this case accounts were to be made up to 25 December to permit lime burners time to collect their money, 21 days credit then being allowed for settlement.

20. The former *Cock with Hen* or *Cock Inn,* Hay, was rented by the Hay Railway to serve as offices.
The passageway on the left of the building led to the company's main wharf in Hay, now the cattle yard.
Photo: Stephen K. Jones (1994)

Dunsford's services were dispensed with on 23 July 1816. The Treasurer was instructed to pay him his salary of £100 to 19 June and £30 'for his services since that period'. Thomas Stephens was paid £30 on account for the erection of the Llanhamlach weigh-house, with a further £70 on 10 December, when presumably the house was ready for Oliver's occupation. Oliver had his own ideas of suitable accommodation, and the December meeting allowed him £11 16s for 'sundry materials added to the house ... and for sundry jobs of work done in and about that house'. James James was paid £4 10s at the same meeting for 'his bill for weighing the articles conveyed along the railway previous to the erection of the weighing-machine at Llanhamlach'. It is not known whether he was an employee of the tramroad company or of the B&A. The cost of the machine and its erection came to £43 1s which was paid on the same day.

By this time it had been decided that the Hay wharf should be sited at the point where the Hay cattle market now stands (SO 22724231) and Hodgkinson was paid £100 for constructing the branch to it from the main tramroad. The site, then known as *The Cock with Hen*, was leased from Viscount Hereford for 21 years from 2 February 1817 at a rental of £64 per annum.[61] This was the site which Ellwood had suggested in his letter to the BBCO. The weighing-machine was to be placed at the junction of the main line and the wharf branch (SO 22454219). The much renovated machine-house still stands on this spot. The branch tramroad can still be traced as it climbs steeply to the wharf, intersected by the line of the later Hereford, Hay & Brecon Railway.

The B&A owned a bank of lime kilns at the Watton (SO 055270), several of which were leased to the BBCO. These were admirably sited for charging with limestone and coal, with the charging mouths actually set in the bank of the

21. The point in Hay at which the branch to the Cock wharf left the main line.
The footpath in the foreground is on the track of the Hay Railway, facing in the direction of Brecon,
while the branch climbs steeply on the left-hand side. Tramway Cottage in the background is the much
reconstructed weigh house of 1817. Photo: P. G. Rattenbury (1979)

canal a few yards only from the water. Burnt lime from the tapping mouths had to be loaded into carts and carried to storage points or to the Hay Railway. To obviate the additional labour of unloading and reloading, the canal Clerk, B. A. Griffiths was instructed on 27 January 1817 to prepare plans and to estimate the cost of making a tramroad from the kilns to the Hay Railway at the point at which it crossed the turnpike road adjacent to the Watton turnpike, a draw-bridge to be used to cross the canal. The application to form the junction was considered by the Hay Railway committee on 26 February and immediately sanctioned, the committee ordering that the necessary tramplates should be lent to the canal company.

Spencer's habit of using his own money to settle the company's debts has already been mentioned. On 26 February 1817 the committee considered a report by a committee which had apparently been appointed by the general meeting to audit his accounts. They had found that all his payments were supported by vouchers with the exception of a few insubstantial amounts for which he had supplied adequate explanations. It was noted that he had paid off several loans (presumably under the Optional Loan scheme) without first obtaining the consent of the committee. It was decided to accept the report, and on the recommendation of the general meeting to sanction the repayments retrospectively. Spencer was thanked for 'his unremitting attention to the interests of this concern' and authorised to continue making payments to Hodgkinson to enable him to complete his contract. He was also authorised to advance money to the workmen who were finishing the wharf and other work at Hay and to account for the sums at the next meeting. A statement of the company's affairs was ordered to be printed and distributed, but it has not been possible to trace a copy. Henry Allen and Hugh Bold were given the task of examining Spencer's bill for the legal expenses which he had incurred and asked to report to the next meeting.

The tramroad was open only as far as Hay, but Hodgkinson had it under active construction thence to Clifford. The problem was, how to pay for a further extension. On 23 June 1817 the committee discussed a resolution from the shareholders that an application for a loan of £8,000 should be submitted to the Exchequer Bill Loan Commissioners as administrators of the Poor Employment Act (57 Geo. III c.34) which had received Royal Assent the previous week.[62] The committee decided that nothing could be done until further details of the scheme were published, but they realised that it would be necessary to supply details of how any money that might be received would be utilised, and Spencer was instructed to ascertain by what amount the company's profits would be likely to benefit from an extension from Clifford to Eardisley. To free him for this work Oliver was to take charge of toll collections until the next general meeting. He was to hand the receipts to Spencer and report on the state of the track and the trade at each committee meeting.

Hay wharf was completed by July 1817 and at the committee meeting held on 30 July it was ordered that spaces there should be let 'in compartments' with all leases to expire on 29 September 1819. On Hodgkinson's report that the tramroad was 'open and passable' from Hay to Clifford Castle (SO 243456) it was resolved that the scale of charges already in force should apply to the new section as well.

Spencer's report was received at this meeting. Whilst it is not given in detail in the minutes, it was obviously in favour of the extension. The final decision had to be that of a general meeting, and

until this could be held Spencer was instructed to obtain the consent of the company's creditors to the application as was required by the Act. In charitable mood the committee authorised a repayment to Jonathan Dixon, George Overton's partner in Brynoer Colliery, of 6d per ton on 107 tons of coal that he had supplied to the Kington Bank during the previous winter for distribution to the poor of Kington.

The *Hereford Journal* of 27 August 1817 carried a notice calling the general meeting for 15 September 1817, stating that the propriety of the company borrowing £8,000 from the Exchequer would then be considered. No report of the proceedings of the general meeting has been seen, but when the committee met on 10 October it had before it a draft of the mortgage of the company's tolls that the Loan Commissioners proposed to take. The draft was approved. Under the scheme the company was to receive eight Exchequer Bills of £1,000 each, and the loan was to be repaid by instalments of £400 per annum plus interest at 5 per cent on the outstanding balances. The draft was returned to the Commissioners for engrossment.

By this time it would have been known that the Kington Railway was being formed to continue the Hay Railway from Eardisley to Kington, and it would be realised that neither company could achieve its full potential unless the Hay Railway was completed to its planned destination. Hodgkinson's estimate of the cost of finishing the railway was accepted by the committee on 10 October 1817, and Spencer was instructed to prepare a contract. The contract price is not stated in the minutes but by looking ahead in the minute book it can be ascertained that Hodgkinson was paid at least £2,400 for the work, although the last payment traced is stated to be 'on account'.[63]

An unexpected charge was authorised for payment on 10 October 1817 when Oliver reported that John Allen, possibly one of the partnership that had surrendered their contract in 1814, had finished raising the roof of 47 yards of the tunnel at a cost of £49 17s. It is not known whether this had been necessitated by some fault in Tipping's workmanship or by subsidence. Further difficulties with the tunnel are indicated by a payment to Oliver on 15 December 1817 of £15 6s 6d for

22. Two views of the Whitney toll bridge. The bridge, which was probably constructed in the early nineteenth century, was used by the Hay Railway to cross the river Wye after attempts at building their own bridge or supplying a ferry had failed.
Photo: Stephen K. Jones (1994)

charges incurred in 'cleansing the rocks from the sides and top of the tunnel and raising the height thereof'. On the same date payment was also made to Howell Maund of Brecon of £9 15s 9d for making and delivering a pair of gates which were to be placed across the tramroad entrance to the Hay wharf.

How the tramroad was to cross the Wye at Whitney had not yet been decided. Spencer reported that he had been negotiating with the proprietors of Whitney bridge for the tramroad to use the existing toll-bridge. The committee considered that the terms proposed were unacceptably high, and that he should again meet the proprietors of the bridge and report to the next

meeting in November if any change had been proposed in the terms. At the meeting on 11 November 1817 it became obvious that the bridge proprietors wanted to farm all the tolls payable at the bridge for a fixed annual sum. The committee resolved that it would be preferable to pay a fixed annual sum for passage over the bridge unless a very much lower farm-rent was demanded.* This meeting received notification that the Exchequer

* It was quite normal for toll-gates and toll-bridges to be let for a fixed annual rent, the 'farmer' hoping to take more in tolls than he expended in rent. Advertisements in the *Hereford Journal* in August 1823 and August 1824 show that at Whitney the lessee could not take tolls for passing tramroad traffic since a fixed annual sum was paid direct to the proprietors in respect of this traffic.

Loan Bills would be handed to Peter Free, banker of Bartholomew Lane, London for onward transmission to John Parry Wilkins at the Brecon Bank.

On 15 December Spencer was reimbursed £575 that he had paid to the Clydach Ironworks for 100 tons of plates, plus £5 15s, the cost of transporting them from Llangynidr to Llangorse Lane to make them readily available at a time when the canal between Llangynidr and Brecon had been under repair. A somewhat belated payment of £10 10s to Benjamin Wanewright was authorised for his survey of the line in Herefordshire in 1811.

Spencer notified the December meeting that Hodgkinson had completed his first contract to construct as far as The Lakes (i.e. Lakes Cottage, so 251465), and it was ordered that traffic should be accepted on the new section 'on payment of the like tonnages as the other parts of the Road'. Hodgkinson reported that he had found that by taking the tramroad alongside the turnpike road from Whitney to Eardisley a saving of eight tons of plates could be made in addition to avoiding the cost of fencing one side of the tramroad, since it would be open to the turnpike. Spencer reported that the Turnpike Commissioners were also in favour as they too would be saved maintenance of fencing on one side of the road, and that they were prepared to advance £50 towards the cost of constructing the tramroad on the new alignment. The one landowner concerned, Tomkyns Dew, also favoured the scheme as the road and tramroad together would require less of his land than if they were constructed separately as under the original plan. Not to be outdone in generosity, the committee offered the Commissioners £50 towards the cost of altering the turnpike – the amount they would be saving on tramplates! Hodgkinson was instructed to prepare estimates of the cost to the company of building its own bridge at Whitney, 'at a height not to impede the navigation of the river', in time for the next meeting. The stipulation in respect of navigation shows that Ellwood's idea of serving Hereford with coal carried to Hay on the tramroad was not as preposterous as might be thought at first glance.

On 20 January 1818 the committee resolved

that it would be 'most advisable' for the company to have their own bridge at Whitney and Spencer was instructed to write to John Urpeth Rastrick of Bridgnorth, asking him to survey the intended site and give his opinion on Hodgkinson's plans. An advance of £500 was made to Spencer to enable him to purchase the plates necessary for the line to Eardisley – with the Exchequer money behind them it was unnecessary to ask him to dip into his own pocket!

Rastrick attended the next committee meeting which was held at the *Boat Inn,* Whitney on 9 February. Having viewed the site of the proposed bridge he stated that he would require further information before he could make a satisfactory report. It was resolved that he should be asked to report on the state of the river; whether he thought that a wooden bridge or a stone bridge would be most suitable; the exact site on which he thought the bridge should be built; and if, in his opinion, a bridge would cost more than the company could afford.

It is possible that a survey made on 26 February on the stability of Whitney bridge was at the instigation of the Hay Railway. Edward Powell of Brecon, the surveyor, confirmed the soundness of the structure in his certificate, stating that in his opinion

… it is not to be injured by anything so far as to be broken down or destroyed unless in a very severe winter great quantities of water should become so great a weight as to force the middle arches.[64]

The survey might also have been made at the behest of the bridge proprietors, anxious to emphasise the soundness of the bridge for use by the tramroad, but it is unlikely to be mere coincidence that on 28 July the tramroad company made a payment of £19 to William Powell to meet 'his bill for surveying measuring and mapping'.

Rastrick's report was considered at the committee meeting of 2 March, including his plan for an iron suspension bridge. It was decided that the cost 'would far exceed the resources of this company' and that

… the plan of a boat or boats for passing the tram waggons over the river Wye is the most advisable to be adopted and that the Clerk make enquiry

23. A waggoner leads his horse past the 22-mile milestone near Whitney on Wye.
This stone remained *in situ* until 1946 when it was removed to Hereford City Museum, where it is now in store.
Drawing: Edward Paget-Tomlinson

respecting the Boat at Chepstow recommended by Mr. Rastrick respecting the necessary machinery.[65]

Sir Charles Morgan, who had considerable landed property in the district around Builth Wells, suggested in separate letters to Hugh Bold and to David Thomas, both solicitors in Brecon, that a branch of the Hay Railway ought to be made to Builth. In his reply, dated 28 February 1818, Bold considered that whilst the terrain was well suited to a tramroad, nine tenths of the population were too poor to use coal 'except at the very lowest price'.[66] Thomas expressed similar views, although he agreed that the branch would be 'of the greatest possible accommodation' to the district. He thought that 'poverty will entirely prevent this part of the world from showing their inclination (by subscription) to further so great a beneficial

improvement'.[67] Both replies illustrate how impoverished were the country and townsfolk of the district.

The Kington Railway, also a plateway, received its Act on 23 May 1818 (58 Geo. III c.63). At its first shareholders' meeting on 2 June a deputation was appointed to attend the Hay company's meeting

… for the purpose of ascertaining if there is any doubt of their completing their Road to Eardisley particularly with reference to crossing the river Wye and for the purpose of obtaining a satisfactory assurance of a limited period for finishing their line.[68]

The Hay company's minutes make no reference to meeting the deputation, but those of the Kington company for 25 July 1818 state that a letter had been received from Spencer suggesting that the deputation should attend on 28 July. Their minutes for 5 September record that the deputation had been given a satisfactory answer.

The alterations to the turnpike road at Whitney cost Tomkyns Dew more than had been anticipated and on 28 June the Hay committee decided that the £50 that they had intended originally to pay to the Turnpike Commissioners should be paid to him instead.

Without waiting for the authority of the committee, on 12 November John Parry Wilkins, the Treasurer, paid the instalment of £400 due to the Exchequer Loan Commissioners plus £400 for interest due to date. On 23 November he was instructed to reimburse himself from the company's funds and was also authorised to pay Spencer £100 for his half-year's salary. On Spencer's own suggestion his salary was reduced to £100 per annum. An advance of £300 was made to Spencer with which he was to purchase plates.

Spencer reported to the committee, also on 23 November, that the tramroad would be open to Eardisley on 1 December 1818 and it was resolved that the existing scale of charges should also apply to the new section.

The Kington Railway was by no means completed at the time and would not be finished for another year, but Hodgkinson was awarded the contract for constructing the connecting line between the two concerns in the sum of £150, with the Hay company finding the land and the track. It is not known why the Hay Railway should have shouldered this responsibility, as the plans for the Kington Railway show it to run right into the Hay company's wharf.[69] Neither minute book gives any reason.

It is probable that the tramroad was opened to Eardisley on 1 December as planned, as on 11 December the committee voted £5 to repay Spencer for his expenditure on coal for distribution to the poor of Eardisley, as was customary on such occasions, and a further £5 in respect of gratuities which he had distributed to workmen on the tramroad.[70]

Obviously some means had been found of crossing the river at Whitney, but it was not until 8 August 1821 that the minute book reveals that the tramroad had been laid over the existing toll-bridge. It records that a payment of £202 6s 1d was to be made 'to Mr. William Longfellow in full for pontage for passing Whitney Bridge from the opening of the Road in 1818 to 1st July 1821'. The meeting also authorised a payment of £83 4s 11d 'for the Boat intended to convey tram carriages over the river at Whitney, and sundry expences in searching for the foundations for a bridge', thus making it apparent that it had been intended at one time to institute a ferry. The minutes do not reveal in what manner this expedient for crossing the river had been found to be impractical.

CHAPTER FIVE

THE HAY RAILWAY
Routine Operations
(1818 – 1833)

WITH its tramroad completed to Eardisley, the Hay company was as yet without the benefit of the anticipated extra traffic from the Kington Railway and still appeared to find difficulty in meeting its engagements. Evidence for this is provided by the delay until 8 August 1821 in payment of pontage due to the proprietors of Whitney bridge which the tramroad had been using since 1818. It can also be seen in the payment of rent on the *Cock with Hen* premises. One and a half years' rent was paid to Viscount Hereford on 17 February 1819; the next payment of a half year's rent due on 2 August 1819 was made on 20 September – perhaps the fact that Lord Hereford was chairman of the company had some bearing on the matter.

By September 1819 the line from Brecon to Hay had been operational for three and a half years, and the state of the track was causing the committee some concern. On 20 September they decided to call on the services of John Llewellin to report on the deficiencies. Llewellin was Agent to Benjamin Hall of the Rhymney Ironworks and Lord of the Manor of Abercarn; he had been in charge of the construction of Hall's Tramroad in the Ebbw valley of Monmouthshire and had been responsible for the extension of the Brinore Tramroad from Trevil to the ironworks in 1815.[71] His report was read to the Hay committee on 8 January 1820. Whilst it was not quoted in detail in the minutes, the following extract from that date indicates that it was not favourable:

The report of Mr. John Llewellin having been read this day and Mr. Hodgkinson having engaged immediately to attend to the objections stated therein and particularly to employ men to put the Road in proper gauge and repair. Ordered that further consideration of the report be postponed until the next meeting and that in view of his neglect to fulfil his present engagement proceedings be immediately taken against him to enforce the performance of his contract and that no further advances of money be made him until the Roads be put in complete repair.

The Kington Railway was nearing completion by now and possibly the thought that their line might not be fit to receive the extra traffic lay behind the panic!

The Kington Railway was opened from Kington to Eardisley on 1 May 1820, by which time it appears that Hodgkinson was back in favour with the committee of the Hay Railway, for on 8 August he was paid £300 in respect of one half year's repairs from 7 November 1819 to 7 May 1820, £100 on account of his contract to make the 200-yard long connecting line between the two tramroads, and £100 on account of his contract to make the line from Hay to Eardisley. He was not paid the remaining £50 for the connecting line until 18 February 1821.

It would appear that the rebate allowed on tonnages for lime-burning coal was being abused. Probably it was being claimed on any small coal that was carried, and on 8 August 1820 the committee decided to recommend to the next general meeting that the privilege be withdrawn, and that until such meeting the regulations should be strictly enforced. It was also decided to recommend that all downward traffic should be

24. A water-colour of Hay, looking south across the river Wye, showing a train of waggons on the stretch between Hay bridge and the Dulas brook, travelling in the direction of Eardisley. By permission of Brecknock Museum, Brecon

subject to a flat rate charge of 3d per ton per mile. After agreeing with Hodgkinson that he should supply the company with blocks weighing not less than 100 pounds the committee ordered that contractors should be supplied with iron sleepers, but it is not known if it was intended that these should be used with the ends resting on the blocks as on the Brinore Tramroad.[72] Finally, Oliver's salary was increased to £100 per annum.

By this time the tramroad was regarded as an integral part of the local landscape, and an advertisement in the *Hereford Journal* of 26 July 1820 for the sale of Tregunter Farm (SO 136339) used the fact that 'the line of Tram Road between Brecon and Hay passes near to this farm, by which coal and lime may be had at a cheap rate' as an inducement to prospective buyers.

On 8 August 1820 Spencer was instructed to advertise for 'a person to keep the fences in repair from the Lakes to Eardisley', and Oliver was ordered to estimate a fair value for the job. The advertisement appeared in the *Hereford Journal* of 6 September 1820, and on 18 September the contract was awarded to Hodgkinson on the same terms as his contract of 18 August 1815 for fencing repairs, viz. £5 per annum per mile. Modern inflation was yet to come!

Under 'The Bye Laws, Orders and Regulations' issued by the company on 11 June 1816 the maximum permitted load for a waggon was fifty hundredweight (2½ tons), *including* the weight of the waggon. In common with other tramroads the Hay Railway experienced considerable difficulty in preventing overloading by the traders, and orders were issued early in 1821 that loads were to be restricted to the permitted weights. This led to the following advertisement appearing in the *Hereford Journal* of 28 February 1821 signed by six traders on the line:

HAY RAILWAY. The public are respectfully informed that in consequence of the reduction in the weight allowed to be carried on this Railway an advance of One Shilling per Ton of coal must necessarily take place at our respective wharves the First of March next.

Hoper Dixon   J. & M. Meredith   John Allen
Sayce & Cheese   Morgan & Bridgwater
Charles Martin
Eardisley, February 24th. 1821

In the next issue of the paper this was followed by a notice signed by Dixon, Morgan & Bridgwater, Allen and the Merediths stating that it was proposed to defer the increase 'until its effect can more clearly be understood'.

The increase in Oliver's salary to £100 granted in August 1820 was due to come into effect on 8 January 1821, but it was not until 6 August 1821 that he was paid £45 for his half year's salary to the previous January and £50 for the half year due 8 July 1821. For him to have carried on it is obvious that he had to use moneys received from tonnages for his private purposes as well as for those of the company, probably accounting to Spencer for his expenditures.

The meeting on 6 August authorised Oliver to charge the company with £10 14s that he had spent on erecting milestones in accordance with the company's Act, and £91 12s 6d for 'erecting a new shed at the tunnel' where there was presumably a wharf serving Talyllyn. The minutes do not make it clear if other payments authorised at this meeting were to reimburse Spencer or Oliver, or if the Treasurer was being instructed to make them. These included £644 for erecting the wharf at Hay, £55 for repairs to the *Cock House*, £18 for making a wharf at Clifford, £151 for a shed at Winforton and £244 for a wharf at Eardisley. From the number of payments for wharves it would seem that Ellwood's fear of too many being provided was in danger of realisation!

The year 1821 saw the last attempt by George Overton to extend the Brinore Tramroad from Talybont on Usk to Talyllyn. In a report accompanying his plans, he stated that up to 2s 6d per ton could be saved on the cost of transporting coal to the Hay Railway, which

… would enable Traders at Talgarth and Three Cocks Yards to sell coal and lime at such prices as would induce all the country from Bronllys to Builth to come to this Railway … instead of fetching them from Brecon.

In all, seven miles of canal and tramroad would be saved.[73] According to a book which he wrote in 1825, the scheme foundered on the opposition of one landowner and the B&A.[74] The true reason for his opposition to the 1812 Act was revealed.

It may have been Overton's suggestion of a

means of reducing the cost of coal along the tramroad that induced the Hay Railway committee to pass a resolution on 8 February 1822 authorising a drawback of one shilling per ton to traders who were prepared to sell best coal at Hay for £1 per ton and lime-coal at 18s per ton, and a further 6d reduction for selling the two grades at Eardisley at £1 3s and £1 1s respectively. There were to be proportional rebates in respect of coal sold at intermediate places. C. R. Clinker [75] states that the rebates were actually allowed, but some doubt is thrown on this by a letter dated 4 March 1822 to Morgan & Bridgwater of Glasbury from the Brecknock Boat Company in response to a request for a reduction in the wholesale price at Brecon which they were unwilling to grant:

> We think it proper to add that it is the opinion of gentlemen more experienced than we are in the business of tramroads that a very particular reduction may be made in the price of haulage at present paid by you and other traders … on the Hay Tramroad.[76]

That there was a certain amount of sharp practice in the coal trade is revealed by a letter from Joseph

25. The east end of the enlarged Talyllyn tunnel adjoining the platforms of the former Talyllyn Junction station. This was possibly the site of the 1821 wharf which served Talyllyn.
Photo: R. A. Cook (*c.*1960)

26. William Bridgwater's stables at Llwynau Bach, Glasbury. Bridgwater was a coal merchant based at Glasbury and one of the leading traders on both the Hay and Kington Railways. The adjoining barn and farmhouse have been converted into a private hotel.
Photo: Stephen K. Jones (1994) by permission of Mr A. Reynolds

Bailey of the Nantyglo Ironworks to John Powell of the BBCo. on 7 March 1822 informing him that

Mr. Powell [William Powell of Powell & Co.] has been here this day and stated that you have been selling coal to a party on the Hay road (usual price of coal at 14s per ton at Brecon) at 12s 6d per ton and in consequence they are compelled to do the same since last Monday which was the time at which they obtained what was your price. It was understood by us when we saw you on Sunday that 13s 6d was the price at Brecon to the Hay road.[77]

Opting out of fixed price agreements is not a modern phenomenon!

The Hay Railway committee continued to endeavour to reduce the price of coal in their attempts to induce a greater trade on their tramroad. On 18 September 1826 the committee learnt that the Pontypool Company would be prepared to sell it in Brecon at 12s 6d per ton if a reduction in canal tonnages could be obtained. In the hope of creating greater competition the tramroad company wrote to the B&A suggesting that it should be possible for them to give a reduction of 1s 4d per ton on coal carried for the whole length of their canal. The proposition was considered at the general meeting of the canal company on 19 Octo-

ber 1826 when it was decided that the canal Act of 1793 required that tonnages should be the same to all comers, and the matter was dropped.[78]

Hodgkinson continued to be employed by the Hay company for a number of years but one gathers that his work was not always particularly satisfactory. On 15 September 1823 the committee minuted that …

… Mr. John Hodgkinson, the contractor, be required to proceed immediately with the repair of such parts of the road as Mr. Oliver has this day reported to be out of repair

and on 26 August 1826, after receiving a report from a Mr Sheasby – the minutes do not identify him further – Hodgkinson was to re-lay and

… fill up the tram road from Brecon to The Lakes … and repair the gates … and also to keep the land and the road in repair in all other respects except re-laying any parts that become defective since Mr. Sheasby's survey.

He was also to repair the Pound Hill and Sheephouse bridges. For this work he was to be paid £100 subject to a satisfactory report by Sheasby.

The minutes of 25 February 1828 make it obvious that Hodgkinson was about to leave the company, since it was agreed that the company should purchase the cottages which he had erected along the line of the tramroad at Oliver's valuation of £166, and that he should be paid £19 in respect of 'sundries left upon the road from Brecon to The Lakes'. For his part Hodgkinson agreed to allow £69

… for certain defective parts of the road exclusive of the Sheephouse Bridge and the Sheephouse embankment, which bridge and embankment Mr. Hodgkinson undertakes to repair to conform with the terms of an agreement and Mr. Sheasby's report.

On 15 September 1828 he was paid £100 for repairs up to 7 November 1826, 'when the Road was taken from him', and repairs became Oliver's responsibility. The last recorded payment to Hodgkinson was on 14 June 1830 when he was paid £45 for repairs done up to 25 March 1830 which was stated to be a final payment. On that date it was reported that Sheephouse bridge had fallen and Oliver was instructed to effect repairs 'so that trade on the road be not impeded'.

From the beginning of his association with the Hay Railway Hodgkinson had been heavily involved in other projects, ranging from the Llanvihangel and Grosmont Railways in Monmouthshire (both of them plateways) in July 1811 to his involvement with the continuation of those lines to Hereford in September 1825, when he was appointed engineer of the Hereford Railway. In 1818 he prepared plans for the Kington Railway, but was rejected as contractor and a year later was the engineer responsible for the Glanyllyn reservoir for the Glamorganshire Canal. In 1825 he was appointed engineer to the Duffryn Llynvi & Porth Cawl Railway (an edge railway) and in 1826 he contracted to construct the Cromford and Sheep Pasture inclines for the Cromford & High Peak Railway. With such a track record obviously he could not apply himself fully to the interests of the Hay Railway, and that supervision of much of the work must have been left to less skilled subordinates.[79]

Spencer was instructed on 16 September 1822 to obtain an estimate for the erection of a weighing-machine at Eardisley 'sufficient for

27. Gravestone of John Hodgkinson in the churchyard of St Woolos' church, Newport (now the cathedral).
Hodgkinson surveyed the Hay Railway, the Kington Railway and many other early lines.
He died at his home, Alteryn House, Newport, on 12 February 1861, aged 88 years.
Photo: Stephen K. Jones (1994)

weighing double tram waggons and farmers' waggons'. It is not clear if it was intended that the machine should be capable of taking two waggons at a time or if it was intended to make special provision for the very small proportion of larger waggons capable of carrying three tons each.[80] It was some time before the machine was operative and it was not until September 1823 that Oliver was instructed to inspect it.

The authorised capital of the Hay Railway was £50,000 under the Act of 1810, but accounts issued in 1823 show that only £42,540 had been received for the original subscriptions. It must be inferred that not all the subscribers had paid their calls in full. There is no record in the committee minutes of any shares being declared forfeit or of any proceedings being taken against defaulters: unfortunately no list of shareholders appears to have survived. It must have come as a pleasant surprise to the committee on 15 September 1823 when it was announced that William Jones had made two payments of £50 as the last calls on his shares. Spencer was ordered to take this amount into the company's general account – a case of better belated than never at all!

John Games was appointed officially as clerk at the Hay machine on 13 September 1824 at a salary of £10 per annum. He appears to have already acted in this capacity for a number of years, as the Treasurer was ordered to pay him £50 'as compensation for his labour in taking note of the tolls at the Hay Machine'.

All the receipts of the company were eventually handed to Spencer who, after paying many creditors, paid the balance to the Treasurer at the Brecon Bank at irregular intervals. On 31 October 1825 it was reported to the committee that he had paid the Treasurer £2,140 and had made payments on the company's behalf amounting to about £1,600. Included in this amount were payments of £53 for arrears of tithes, £59 for rates due in the various parishes through which the tramroad passed, £300 to Homfray & Co. of Tredegar Ironworks for plates, including £48 for the special channel-section plates used across Whitney bridge. As Spencer had paid £2 especially for carriage on the latter items, it must be assumed that they were needed urgently. Repairs of the

branch to the Hay wharf had cost £259, and among the smaller sums listed in the minutes were payments of £6 6s to John Jones for 'triangular scales' and £10 2s for a measuring wheel and carriage. Spencer had paid himself his salary of £100 and had paid Oliver £250 in respect of two and a half years' salary. It was fortunate for Oliver that he handled large amounts of the company's money and could advance himself sufficient for his day-to-day needs. The company's bank account must have looked fairly healthy, as payments were ordered of £500 to Tomkyns Dew, £66 to William Wellington, and £120 to the executors of William Maddy in respect of interest. The minutes do not state if the original sums had been lent under the Optional Loan scheme or at some other time.

Although the company's bye-laws forbade hauliers from riding on their waggons, it appears that by 1826 it had become commonplace for passengers to be carried, and on 26 August the committee ordered

That the Clerk collect and receive from all Persons travelling in tram-carts six pence for every such Person six miles and two pence for every other traveller and so in proportion …

which may have been perfectly clear to those present at the meeting but is most puzzling to those of us who were not so favoured. There is no record of the company ever having paid Passenger Duty.[81]

The Hay Railway was not a common carrier and functioned solely as the owner of a specialised form of turnpike on which the public was entitled to carry in suitable vehicles, employing their own hauliers and means of haulage and paying tonnages which varied with the weight and nature of the goods carried. Anxious to exploit any means of increasing its receipts, on 18 September 1826 the committee authorised £100 to be spent in constructing waggons for hire to traders on the line. In the accounts which Spencer submitted on 15 September 1828 he showed the sum of £102 7s as the cost of the exercise. The experiment does not appear to have been successful as in September 1829 Oliver was instructed to have the waggons repaired – evidently some had seen some use – and then to sell them.

The company had not settled its debt to Spencer by 15 September 1828 on which date the minutes record that, in all, he had made payments to a total of £8,038 6s 11d, including such sums as £543 for six and a half years' pontage at Whitney, £448 for seven years' rent of the *Cock with Hen*, and £686 in respect of the interest payments ordered on 31 October 1825. The minutes also record that he was owed £474 9s for legal fees, probably those arising from the company's land transactions. It is not known if William Longfellow, the owner of Whitney bridge, and Viscount Hereford, the owner of the *Cock* premises, had been paid the large lump sums quoted or had been paid as the pontage and rent became due. Oliver seems to have been given the somewhat onerous task of sorting out the company's affairs *vis-à-vis* Spencer. Oliver reported that the company owed Spencer £634 16s in respect of interest arising on moneys paid by him on the company's behalf up to December 1821. The committee sanctioned payment of this amount, but in order to spread the load payment was to be made by promissory notes of unspecified tenors.

After ordering that the accounts should be printed and circulated to the proprietors,[82] the committee considered difficulties that had arisen with the track, and ordered that Bye-Law no. 2 should be strictly enforced. This stated that 'No waggon shall be permitted to pass on this Railway the Wheels and Axles of which are not fitted to the Gage [*sic*] of the Rails', and added a clause that it should be the duty of the weigh-house clerks not to

... suffer any Tram Waggons to pass along the Road after 31st. December next unless the Axle Trees of the Wheels be at least Three feet and One inch asunder ...

thereby ensuring that the whole weight of the waggon and its load should not be borne on one pair of three feet plates.

The price at which coal was sold on the line of the tramroad had a direct bearing on the quantity sold, which was reflected in the receipts for tonnages. On 7 January 1829 Spencer wrote to the BBCo. suggesting that unless the wholesale price at Brecon was reduced 'the Forest [of Dean] coal will find its way to the Hay – it has already found its

way to Kington and the country', and warning that should the country trade be lost it could only be ascribed to the high prices charged.[83] A year later Benjamin Trusted of Hay wrote to the BBCo. pointing out that whilst they had reduced their prices at Llangattock and Llangynidr wharves, at Brecon, whence the Hay trade was supplied, there had been no reduction. This was causing difficulties to those trading on the tramroad, 'as it is only such as would or must have credit will buy from us'. Other customers preferred to send carts to the cheaper source of supply.[84] It would be interesting to know by what route Kington was supplied from the Forest of Dean.

Oliver had assumed responsibility for the maintenance of the tramroad in 1826, and by 1830 he had also taken over a number of Spencer's duties. On 8 March 1830 he was instructed to pay Walter Churchey, a Brecon solicitor, £50 for a half year's pontage due to William Longfellow, and £544 to the Commissioners for Exchequer Loans in payment of an instalment of the loan plus interest, and to draw £891 6s from the Treasurer to pay interest due on the company's promissory notes. The only bad debt recorded in the minutes was dealt with at this meeting when George Coleman was 'exonerated from any further demands by the Company on his paying 5s in the pound on the amount of the Company's demand for tonnages'.

J. & J. W. Meredith of Kington Foundry were, as far as is known, the only traders on the tramroad who dealt in both iron and coal, and there is no doubt that the following minute of 17 September 1829 was aimed at them:

That the waggons now used for carrying iron upon the railway be permitted to continue so long as they do not carry any coal, but that no more waggons of that construction be suffered to pass upon the road unless the wheels are of the same gauge as those of the other waggons.

It is not known in what way the waggons were defective, unless, due to constant use the wheels had acquired what is known in motoring circles as 'negative camber', and were thus too wide for the track.

Two other decisions of the meeting are of interest in relation to traffic working. One ordered that hauliers should use shafts on the leading waggons instead of the usual chains, presumably to ensure that the horses walked in the middle of the track and could be used to restrain waggons on the downhill sections. The second stipulated that no more than eight waggons should be allowed to follow each other. It would appear that the custom had arisen of coupling waggons together in trains hauled by more than one horse, and that the passing places were not long enough to accommodate more than eight waggons without fouling the partings at either end.

How things had changed financially was revealed on 21 September 1829, when it was reported that Spencer owed the company £1,426. The chairman was ordered to draw bills of exchange on him for this sum, and also to draw £710 from the Treasurer to pay interest on the Optional Loan and other outstanding promissory notes. From this time on it was the usual procedure for cheques to be drawn on the bankers and the money to be handed to Oliver for distribution, thus further removing control of the company's finances from Spencer.

On 14 June 1830 it was reported that Spencer was again indebted to the company, this time to the tune of £700 after allowing for a payment of £577 that had been made to the Commissioners. The committee accepted his undertaking to repay this by the end of July. It was also reported to the meeting that Sheephouse bridge had actually fallen, and Oliver was instructed to have it repaired 'by erecting substantial side-walls and putting an iron platform on the railway'. On 13 September he was authorised to draw the £53 9s 6d that it had cost.

This September meeting authorised payment to John Games of £10 in respect of his year's salary to the previous December. His days at the Hay machine were numbered, however, when Oliver was instructed to employ a 'suitable person' to examine the machine to see if it could be repaired or would have to be scrapped. Oliver was further authorised to employ a clerk at the machine at a salary not exceeding £20 per annum with free accommodation.

Many canal and tramroad Acts contained clauses that obliged the company to carry materials for the repair of roads free of charge: the Hay Railway was an exception, but on 13 December 1830 the committee authorised the proprietors of Whitney bridge

… to convey stone for the repair of the roadway and the raising of the road on the south side of the bridge from the waste at Clifford to the bridge toll free …

but ordained specifically that it should be on this occasion only.

At their meeting on 13 December the committee appointed Oliver to be 'collector of tolls', thereby further eliminating Spencer's control over the company's finances – previously Oliver had handed over all takings to Spencer. Another innovation at this meeting was the appointment of Hugh Bold and Tomkyns Dew to audit the accounts for the past year in time to report to the general meeting.

The report on the Hay machine was unfavourable and Oliver was ordered 'to bespeak a double weighing machine to be erected at the house near Hay so as to weigh two waggons at one time', but no limit was placed on the cost. Starting at this meeting it seems that the pontage at Whitney had been arranged to be a flat £100 per annum and regular payments of £50 per half year are recorded thereafter.

Oliver submitted his resignation to the committee on 12 September 1831, 'as soon as a suitable person can be found to take his place', and Spencer was instructed to insert advertisements in the papers for a person 'thoroughly conversant with engineering and the value of work'. It was reported to this meeting that William Bridgwater, probably the largest coal trader on the tramroad, owed £275 12s for tonnages that should have been paid in the previous June. The chairman was authorised to draw a bill of exchange on him to clear the debt.

By 15 October an application had been received for Oliver's position from William Wells. Spencer was instructed to make enquiries as to his 'integrity, sobriety and capacity'. From the fact that these were to be made to Thomas Cooke, the Clerk to the Monmouthshire Canal, Jones & Waddington of Usk, that company's solicitors, and E. H. Phillips, a banker of Pontypool and a member of the MCC committee, it would appear that Wells was an employee of that company. The MCC minutes mention several employees of the same name and it has been impossible to find which one was concerned in this case. On 5 November the committee decided that Wells' references were unsatisfactory, and ordered that he should be informed 'that another person will be chosen'. Spencer was instructed to offer the position of 'Superintendend [*sic*] of the Line' to Stephen Bowen Jones of Swansea and to inform him that a bond of £1,000 would be required. His salary was to be the same as Oliver's had been, viz. £112 per annum with living accommodation provided at Llanhamlach.

On 22 February 1832 Spencer was instructed to obtain the requisite signatures to call a special general meeting of the proprietors to discuss a reduction in tonnages so as to stimulate trade on the line. At the same time they viewed with disquiet the fact that unpaid tonnages amounted to £620. It was resolved to allow traders fourteen days to pay up or face prosecution.

The *Hereford Journal* of 29 February carried the notice calling the meeting for 29 March over the signatures of Henry Allen, Tomkyns Dew and Sir George Cornewall. No report of the meeting has been seen and it is not known whether any reductions were made.

The minutes for 10 September 1832 record the payment of £84 for nine months' salary to S. B. Jones of £84 and a payment to Thomas Perks of £20 for one year's salary as 'machine minder at Hay', and it must be assumed that he had been appointed to replace John Games. The minutes for 2 April 1833 record a payment of £50 to Spencer as his year's salary, but no minute has been found recording a reduction from £100 per annum. The company's accounts for the year ended September 1833, however, show the amount paid for salaries to have been £182,[85] which can be broken down into £112 for Jones, £50 for Spencer and £20 for Perks. The only later accounts to have been seen record the same total amount for salaries, but apart from Spencer it is not known if the recipients were the same.[86]

The last entry in the only minute book known to have survived records that Jones was to draw on the Treasurer for £327 2s with which to pay the interest due on the company's promissory notes for one year. This would mean that £6,542 was still outstanding of the £6,805 originally raised under the Optional Loan scheme.

CHAPTER SIX

THE HAY RAILWAY
Later History
(1833 – 1863)

ETAILED history of the Hay Railway comes to an end with the last entry on 10 June 1833 in the only minute book which is known to have survived, and only sketchy details are available from then on. Each September from 1834 until 1843 notices calling general meetings of the proprietors continued to appear in the *Hereford Journal,* but there is no record of the outcome of any meeting in subsequent issues.

An advertisement appeared in the issue of 7 October 1835 offering for sale seven shares in the company, and on 17 December seventeen shares were advertised for sale. On each occasion application was to be made to a 'Mr. Pemberton, solicitor, Hay (if by letter – post paid)'. No clue is given as to the identity of the owner of the shares, and in view of the fact that the capital was not fully subscribed it is possible that these were shares which had been forfeited for non-payment of calls, and were offered by the company.

The final instalment of the Exchequer Loan, due in December 1837, was probably made on time, and a start was then made on the repayment of the Hay Railway Optional Loan and other promissory notes that had been issued. At the last meeting recorded in the minutes the amount authorised to be paid for interest on the notes was £327 2s, indicating that notes to the value of £6,542 were still in circulation,[87] £305 of the original loan having already been repaid. The odd £42 of the outstanding amount was accounted for by a note issued to Thomas Brown on 23 November 1818 in payment for land, and apparently taken over by Spencer before 1831 and then treated by him as a loan to the company.

The gas works at Hay started production on 14 December 1840,[88] and it was probably about this time that the Hay Railway set up a wharf on the north of the town (SO 23054277), adjacent to the site of the later railway station. This wharf had only limited importance, as is shown by comparing its rateable value with that of the wharf in the town. The former was valued at a mere £6 per annum, the latter at £80 per annum.[89]

There was an attempt to introduce mechanical transport over the Kington and Hay Railways on 8 March 1841 when two men took a vehicle worked through gearing by crank handles from Kington to Brecon at a reputed speed of six miles an hour. Setting off from Brecon at 5 o'clock on the next day, carrying a ton of coal on the vehicle, to do the return journey, they had reached the 'Gas-House' at Hay when the necessity for refreshment overcame them. The contraption was left on the track for some time, during which some local youths interfered with the machine, breaking one of the gears, with the result that instead of reaching Kington that night, the travellers could only get as far as Eardisley by the following morning, and that by pushing their vehicle.[90]

As far as can be ascertained, the only fatal accident recorded from the actual running of the Hay Railway occurred on 4 September 1843, when a train of waggons running down from the Cock wharf to the main line by gravity struck and killed an elderly woman who was crossing the incline by a public path. At the subsequent inquest the fact that no-one was attempting to control the waggons was particularly stressed.[91]

The company's promissory notes had nearly been paid off in full by March 1841. Philip Vaughan, Sir Charles Morgan's Agent, notified him that the company was prepared to repay the last note held by him for £300, and asked that the note should be forwarded to him to be surrendered to the company.[92] Morgan had originally lent £875 and was now to be repaid in full. The accounts for June 1843 show that in that year notes for £275 were repaid, leaving an indebtedness on that account of £150 only.[93]

Following the success of the Liverpool & Manchester Railway, opened in 1830, there were a number of schemes for railways in the Usk valley. Although several schemes proposed to use the line of the B&A as the basis for their lines, none would have affected the Hay Railway until in 1845 the Welsh Midland Railway from Birmingham to Swansea was proposed, with branches to local towns including Brecon and Hay.[94] To reach Brecon the promoters proposed to purchase the B&A for £182,000, and a deposit of £18,200 was paid. The WMR offered to purchase the Hay Railway for £45,000, which Vaughan advised Morgan on 29 May 1845 had been accepted provisionally.[95] The same letter records that in the previous year

28. The bridge which carried the Hay Railway over the Dulas brook at Hay.
The southern, or right-hand bank of the stream is in Wales, the northern in England. Hay gasworks lay on the Welsh side of the bridge. The site is now occupied by modern houses, the wall of one of which can be seen on the extreme right. Newport Street wharf was on the English side, between the tramroad and the road to Hereford.
Photo: Stephen K. Jones (1994)

29. The incline to the Cock wharf at Hay, constructed in 1817, climbs alongside the wall.
The main line of 1816, in the direction of Eardisley, follows the footpath to the left. The only recorded
fatal accident on the Hay Railway occurred on this incline in 1843.
Photo: P. G. Rattenbury (1979)

the Hay Railway had paid a dividend of one per cent, 'and the prospects are poor'. On 10 June Vaughan informed Morgan that he had attended the Hay meeting at which it had been decided to accept the WMR offer subject to their taking a lease of the tramroad for two years at £1,000 per annum.[96] On 14 June he told him that his thirty shares, plus the five held by his brother, the Rev. Augustus Morgan, 'should realise £2,100 to the Welsh Midland'.[97]

Vaughan's arithmetic would appear to have been rather faulty, as the Hay Railway accounts show that the original subscriptions amounted to £42,540, to raise which at least 426 shares must have been in issue. The £45,000 offered by the WMR, divided among 426 shares, would mean that they were worth £105 12s 8d each, which would have made the Morgan shares worth some £3,697 in total. Vaughan's valuation of £2,100 for the 35 shares meant that they were worth only £60 each, and the whole 426 shares worth £25,560,

which would mean that there were undisclosed debts of £19,440.

The decisive meeting of the tramroad proprietors was called for 27 November 1845, a notice to this effect being inserted in the *Hereford Journal*.[98] The matters to be discussed included the letting of the tolls for 'two whole years', the terms of the suggested lease, and

… that the Proprietors may take into consideration the propriety of dismissing from their respective offices and appointments the Clerk to the said Company … the Superintendent and Collector of Tonnages and such other officers of … the Hay Railway Company as they … in their discretion may think fit.

It is a great pity that no report of the proceedings appeared in any subsequent issues of the paper.

The WMR failed to obtain its Act[99] and any resolution that the meeting may have passed can have had little significance for future events.

James Spencer resigned from his position as

Clerk in 1847 on his imprisonment for debt. He had been committed to Hereford jail for his failure to hand over the moneys of the Gwynn Charity of which he was a trustee. He died in prison in 1851 at the age of eighty-five. His unorthodox book-keeping methods had probably caught up with him. One is left to wonder whether those who called the meeting of 27 November 1845 had some inside knowledge of the way in which the wind was blowing.[100] Spencer was succeeded as Clerk to the Hay Railway by his partner, Thomas James, who continued in office until the dissolution of the company.

There is no doubt that several dividends were paid between 1842 and 1847 but no details have been found. Writing to Walter Maybery, who had succeeded to the solicitors' practice of Jones & Powell of Brecon, on 27 May 1847, Thomas James informed him that at a general meeting on 24 May it had been decided to waive the penalty of £1 that the Act ordained should be imposed on proprietors who failed to attend meetings, either in person or by proxy. This sum had been deducted by the Treasurer when paying dividends to Maybery as the personal representative of William Wilkins, deceased, before the meeting had been held. James enquired if Maybery was now the owner of the shares, and if so, requested him to forward details of when and how they had come into his possession in order that the register of shareholders might be brought up to date. His letter continued:

Miss Frances Wilkins had one share on which four of the dividends declared have been paid. I believe she is now dead – are you entitled to her share or can you tell me who is? [101]

Besides revealing that dividends had been paid the letter shows that the share register was by no means up to date, and that James was having difficulty in filling the gaps left by Spencer's slap-dash methods.

On 10 January 1849 the Kington Railway decided to reduce its tonnages on house coal by ¾d per ton per mile on condition that the Hay Railway reduced their charge on the commodity by ¼d per ton per mile and that the coal traders reduced the price of best coal at Kington to 29s per ton. It appears that there was an increase in the quantity of coal carried from Eardisley to Kington as a result and on 3 November the Kington Railway decided on a further reduction of ¼d per ton per mile subject to the Hay Railway making an equal reduction.[102] On 12 January 1852 the proprietors of the Kington Railway received a delegation from the Hay Railway who suggested that both companies should introduce a flat rate of 1d per ton per mile on coal, provided that the B&A would fall in with the suggestion of the same charge being made on the canal, as had already been proposed to them by the Hay Railway. The Kington Railway refused to give an answer immediately, but a week later decided that the proposal could not be entertained. The Clerk was instructed to 'write Mr. Perks accordingly'.[103] Despite this refusal the Hay Railway wrote to the B&A on 24 January, but the canal company also turned down the suggestion.[104]

From the mention of 'Mr. Perks' in the Kington Railway's resolution of 19 January it appears that by this time S. B. Jones had left the service of the Hay Railway and that T. C. Perks, the former weigh-house clerk at Hay, had succeeded him, perhaps under the resolution of November 1845, although there is no direct evidence on this point.

The Hay Railway again approached the B&A on 27 April 1854 with the suggestion that both the tramroad and the canal should institute a tonnage of 1d per ton per mile on coal. This time the B&A considered the point worthy of consideration and instructed their Clerk to convene a special general assembly to make a decision. None of the canal proprietors attended the meeting, which was called for 10 August, and the matter went by default.[105]

Following the demise of the Welsh Midland Railway scheme there were a number of suggestions for railways to Brecon which would have used the canal in whole or in part,[106] but it was not until July 1854 that a proposal arose which would have superseded the Hay Railway. That month a meeting of the 'county' in Brecon, under the chairmanship of Lord Hereford,[107] formed a committee to promote the Leominster, Hay & Brecon Railway.[108] A subscription was opened in September and £48,000 was promised.[109] A meeting at Hay on 6 October was informed that the estimated cost of the line would be £185,000.[110]

Notice of intent to apply for a Bill was published in the *Hereford Journal* of 15 November, but in its following issue the paper announced that it had been decided not to proceed with the scheme due to insufficient support. A meeting of the Hay Railway proprietors called for 1 December in support was adjourned *sine die*.[111]

As early as January 1837 a prospectus had appeared for a railway from Brecon to Merthyr Tydfil surveyed by Edward Powell of Birmingham. The time was not ripe, however, for so ambitious a project and the scheme was stillborn.[112] The *Hereford Journal* of 3 March 1841 announced a further attempt to unite the two towns by means of a tunnel from the Usk valley through to Merthyr which might have been feasible had modern methods of tunnelling been available, but which was well beyond the means of the time. Interest was again aroused when the Welsh Midland Railway was suggested and an amalgamation of the two companies was proposed which, of course, fell through on the failure of the WMR to obtain an Act.[113]

The idea of a railway to Merthyr was revived in 1836 when John Parry de Winton* and a Brecon solicitor, J. R. Cobb, engaged Henry Conybeare of London to re-survey the route to Merthyr.[114] A prospectus was issued in October 1858 naming J. P. de Winton as chairman and Conybeare and his partner Birkinshaw as engineers,[115] and an Act was obtained in August 1859 for a railway from Pant, near Dowlais, to Talybont on Usk. At Talybont it was intended to continue to Brecon over the lines of the proposed Breconshire Railway & Canal Co. This company had been promoted by the Newport, Abergavenny & Hereford Railway and some of the committee members of the B&A with the intention of running on the line of the canal from Abergavenny to Brecon. Unfortunately for the Brecon & Merthyr Tydfil Junction Railway the BR&CC Bill which was before the House in the same Session failed to become an Act, and the B&M was left with no means of reaching Brecon.

Plans were also afoot to provide Brecon with

railway communication from the north. Early in 1857 Captain the Hon. Walter Devereux, RN, of Tregoyd, proposed a railway from Hereford to Brecon to William Field (a partner of the railway contractor, Thomas Brassey, who was at the time contemplating the Leominster & Kington Railway) and David Thomas of Brecon, the solicitor to the Brinore Tramroad. Throughout 1857–8 meetings, which were seemingly well supported, were held in all the small towns lying on the proposed route,[116] but in such a rural district enthusiasm was not matched by subscriptions. Devereux was anxious that the line should be financed by local money to avoid control by London financiers,[117] but by September 1858 he had withdrawn from active participation in the scheme, and the prospectus issued in September 1859 shows strong London influence.[118] This prospectus shows that from Eardisley to Hay and Glasbury the intended railway followed the line of the Hay Railway; but as there were visions of continuing to Milford Haven when the time was ripe, it followed very much the line of Crosley's original plan for the Hay Railway from Glasbury to Brecon, where, instead of joining the canal, a terminus well to the north of the town was proposed in preparation for the westward extension.

By the beginning of 1859 it had become clear that the local people were not interested in an extension beyond Brecon, and Thomas informed a meeting at Hereford on 23 February that 'it would be for those between Brecon and Swansea to make the connecting link'. He had no doubt that with that incubus out of the way the Herefordians would be more ready to subscribe the £45,000 necessary for the plan to proceed, which would make Hereford 'scarcely second to any city in the kingdom'.[119]

The Hereford, Hay & Brecon Railway's Bill received its third reading in the Commons on 25 April 1859, and Royal Assent was given on the same day as that for the B&M, 1 August 1859 (22–33 Vic. c.84). The Act gave no authority to use any part of the Hay Railway without that company's expressed permission given under the company's common seal. It did, however, impose a duty on the HH&B to ensure that the owners of Whitney bridge should receive a minimum income of £345 per annum.

---

* A branch of the banking family of Wilkins changed their name to de Winton in 1839.

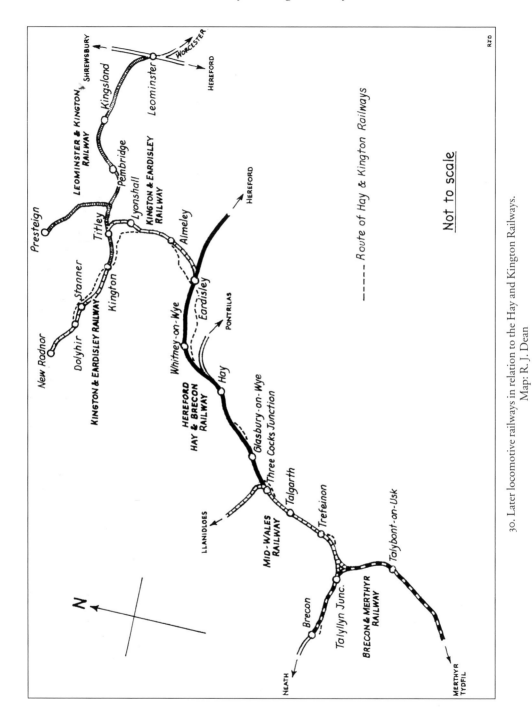

30. Later locomotive railways in relation to the Hay and Kington Railways.
Map: R. J. Dean

While it does not appear to have been part of the original intention of the HH&B to purchase the Hay Railway, the *Hereford Journal* of 27 April 1859 reported that at a meeting of the subscribers David Thomas had stated that he appreciated that the Hay Railway had offered no opposition to their Bill and that the railway would be prepared to offer a fair value for the tramroad company's shares. Obviously he thought that the valuation of the shares would be very low for, whilst a dividend of 10s per £100 share had been paid in 1857, no dividend had been declared at the 1858 general meeting.

A meeting of the Hay Railway shareholders was held on 25 May 1859 at which Thomas revealed what the HH&B was prepared to offer, but no conclusions were reached and the meeting was adjourned to 6 June when it was decided to sell the Hay Railway at £20 per £100 share, and a draft agreement was signed under which the Hay company was exonerated from any expenses in the transfer.[120] It is interesting to note that both Devereux and Perks attended these meetings as shareholders in the Hay Railway.

That the line of the Hay Railway was not to be followed was brought up at a meeting of the HH&B on 10 October 1859 at what was now the *Swan Hotel* in Hay. A Dr R. Bowen stated that it was on the understanding that the railway would pass through Talgarth that many subscriptions from that town had been obtained; he thought that to omit such an important place from the scheme was an error. The meeting was told by David Thomas that to make a deviation through Talgarth would mean that two additional miles of railway would be necessary as well as the construction of a tunnel to get to Brecon, the cost of which would be an extra £26,000. Had they listened to all the suggested inclusions in the line 'instead of the line being 34 miles long it would be about 72 miles and adopt a zig-zag direction'[121] – an obvious exaggeration but one that made a point!

On the same day that the HH&B and the B&M were granted their Acts the Mid Wales Railway was authorised to build a line from Llanidloes to Newbridge on Wye. The company's original request had been for a line from Llanidloes to Llandovery, but the same session of Parliament had preferred that the latter place should be served by the Central Wales Railway, and had cut the Mid Wales proposal to a line ending at Newbridge. Thus, in common with the B&M, the MWR was left without a suitable terminus.[122] Notice of intent to continue their railway to Three Cocks was published in the *Hereford Journal* of 16 November 1859, and plans for a line from Newbridge to Talyllyn were deposited on 30 November.[123]

16 November 1859 was also the day on which the B&M chose to publish its intention of continuing from Talybont on Usk to a point in the parish of Llanvihangel-Talyllyn 'three furlongs or thereabouts east of the east end of the tunnel of the Hay Railway'. On the same day, too the HH&B published its intention of applying to Parliament for an Act to enable it to purchase the Hay Railway and to use such parts as it required for its own railway.[124] The Hay Railway had become the focus of all attempts at making railways to Brecon, for the B&M plans deposited on 30 November also showed its destination to be that town.[125]

That the HH&B was contemplating the abandonment of its line through Bronllys was revealed at its general meeting on 7 February 1860 in a statement that the contractors who had been engaged, M'Cormick & Holmes, considered that a large saving could be effected in the line from Hay to Brecon. The contractors were reported to be so certain of the success of the line that they were prepared to accept one third of their cost of construction, amounting to £221,000, in shares in the company. The directors were in negotiation with the newly formed West Midland Railway to work the HH&B at 4 per cent of the latter's paid up capital as soon as twenty miles of line were ready for traffic. Hints were also let fall that the directors still had ideas of continuing to Milford Haven.[126]

A promotional meeting of the MWR at Merthyr on 28 April 1860 strongly urged the advisability of the MWR making a junction at Talyllyn with the B&M.[127] This was only to be expected in a town strongly in support of the B&M, but at a meeting at Brecon on 3 May the contrary opinion, that the railway should finish at Three Cocks, was expressed, there being many supporters of the HH&B in the gathering.[128] The *Hereford Journal* of 7 April 1860 reported that the preamble of the MWR Bill had been approved in the Commons, and in its issue of 26 June it reported that, in spite of opposition from the HH&B in the Lords, the Bill had received its third reading on 21 June.

Both the MWR and the B&M were naturally worried lest, once the HH&B had acquired the whole of the Hay Railway, they would put an exorbitant price on the parts which the two companies would require. The B&A had other grounds for worry. By 1869 the Monmouthshire Canal Company had converted all its tramroads to railways, and no amount of rate cutting by the B&A would have brought the traffic of the iron trade back to them. Thus it had to rely solely on such traffic as was to be had in coal and lime to Brecon for onward transmission by the Hay Railway. On 1 February 1860 the canal committee decided to petition against the HH&B Bill on the grounds that

31. Mid Wales Railway boundary marker, formerly located at Talyllyn West junction, where the Mid Wales Railway joined the Brecon & Merthyr Railway. At this point the MWR and the B&MR successively used the trackbed of the Hay Railway. Photo: C. R. Clinker collection, Brunel University Library (*c.*1960)

at no point would the railway approach within three-quarters of a mile of the canal, whereas the Hay Railway ran into a canalside wharf. Should the HH&B not be completed, either through lack of funds or for any other reason, once they had purchased the Hay Railway, traffic between Brecon and the Wye valley would be completely at a standstill.[129] The B&M also lodged a petition on the grounds that the part of the Hay Railway required by them under their Bill, which had already been deposited, was not needed by the HH&B as shown on its plans.[130] The canal company was not so worried where the B&M was concerned, as J. R. Cobb had given an undertaking that the railway would construct a siding to the canal at Talybont[131] – a promise that was never fulfilled.

The HH&B Bill passed all its stages in the Commons by the middle of April 1860, and in accordance with the Standing Orders of the House of Lords, the willingness of the proprietors of the Hay Railway to sell had to be confirmed at a general meeting, which was to be held on 21 May. Giving a résumé of the events prior to the meeting, the *Hereford Times* of 26 May reminded its readers that at a previous meeting the Hay Railway shareholders had agreed to sell their concern to the HH&B 'for something over £8,000', and that

… It appears that at the time the Hay Company agreed to get rid of their tramway for this sum a considerable number of the proprietors were not aware that two other railway companies would probably require to adopt other portions of it; … it now appears that these two companies require upwards of eight miles of this tramway and the consequence is that a considerable section of the proprietors refused to sanction the preliminary arrangements entered into for the transfer of the tramway to the Hereford and Brecon Company … The Hay meeting on Monday was, in consequence, much more numerously attended than it has probably been since the foundation of the company … But Alas! … By some unaccountable error, whilst the advertisements in the newspaper convened the meeting to be held in the Swan Hotel, the circulars issued to the shareholders summoned them to the Town Hall … the consequence was that the legal gentlemen present declared that the meeting was *void ab initio* and no resolution carried could be held to be in compliance with Standing Orders.

32. The west end of Talyllyn tunnel, as enlarged and converted for use by the Brecon & Merthyr Railway in 1863. Construction of the earlier tramroad tunnel started in 1812. The tunnel mouth is still visible (1994) although the approaches are much overgrown and waterlogged.
Photo: R. A. Cook (*c.*1960)

There was considerable discussion as to what the meeting could or could not do, and it was eventually decided to turn it into an ordinary meeting of the Hay Railway shareholders, a number of whom had travelled from London and Shrewsbury, at which it might be possible to reconcile the opposing factions present.

The meeting became somewhat heated and David Thomas said that the shareholders should, in all honesty, confirm the previous arrangement. He complained bitterly of the conduct of J. R. Cobb who had now decided to oppose the deal. Captain Devereux, in his capacity as a Hay Railway shareholder, stated that it was only that day that he had heard of the interest of the other two railways, and he felt that information had been withheld deliberately. If the whole tramroad should pass to the HH&B it could be used to impede the progress of the other companies and it would be possible for them to impose far higher costs. Cobb thought that the HH&B should reveal what sum they intended to extract from the other

railways, and that this should have been incorporated into the Bill. R. S. France, the Secretary of the Mid Wales line, stated that it was his opinion that the HH&B only wanted the line from Three Cocks to Talyllyn taken from his company in order that they might make it for themselves. This was confirmed when Shepherd, of Smith & Shepherd, the HH&B solicitors, agreed that it was possible that his company might want this section for their own purposes. The Rev. H. de Winton thought that, as planned, the HH&B had adopted the worst possible line into Brecon, one which would swallow much of their capital, and that the line of the MWR was infinitely preferable; if the HH&B intended to inhibit the progress of the other lines by adopting 'this dog-in-the-manger attitude', he thought the Hay Railway shareholders would be justified in renouncing their bargain. The same issue of the paper carried a notice for a further meeting to be held on 18 June at the *Swan Hotel*.

On 20 June the *Hereford Journal* published a special supplement stating that the 'struggle'

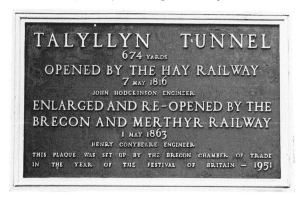

33. Commemorative plaque, formerly located at Talyllyn Junction station.
Photo: R. A. Cook (*c.*1960)

between the MWR, the B&M and the HH&B for the absolute possession of the Hay Railway had terminated with the HH&B obtaining more than three-fourths of the votes in its favour.

The Hay Railway Act (23–24 Vic. c.179) received the Royal Assent on 6 August 1860. The preamble stated that the capital of the Hay Railway consisted of 428 shares in issue, all fully paid, to a value of £42,800, and acknowledged that the MWR and B&M both required to use parts of its route. By section 12 the HH&B was to allot two of its shares for each Hay Railway share to those willing to accept payment by this means; those requiring to be paid in cash were to receive £20 per share. Whichever alternative was chosen all Hay Railway shareholders were to receive £2 8s per share in cash, representing interest at 4 per cent on £20 from 6 June 1859, the date of the original agreement, to 5 June 1862, the date on which the Act ordained that the deal should be completed. Sections 28 and 29 authorised the B&M and the MWR respectively to enter on such parts of the Hay Railway as were required for their lines. That the petition lodged by the B&A had had some influence on the Parliamentary discussions was shown by section 26 which laid down that the tramroad was not to be taken out of use between the public wharf of the B&A at Brecon

… and the point on such Railway Three furlongs South-Eastward of Hay Bridge [i.e. the wharf at Hay] … unless there shall be provided either over

the Hay Railway or other means of Railway Communication between the Wharf and the before-mentioned Point.

No contemporary record has been found as to how this provision was accomplished, but Barrie records that Conybeare, the B&M engineer, was complaining in 1862 of the difficulties which he was experiencing in enlarging Talyllyn tunnel to railway standards with the tramroad still in use.[132]

Neither the B&M nor the MWR felt that they could rely on the bona fides of the HH&B and that the time that was to elapse before the company was to finalise the purchase was too long. Both companies consequently obtained Acts in 1861 in virtually identical terms authorising them to treat with either the HH&B or the Hay Railway should the purchase not have been completed, and to enter on the land required immediately on the passage of the Acts.[133]

The B&M was opened to Brecon on 1 May 1863, by which time all Hay Railway traffic through Talyllyn tunnel must have ceased, and the MWR commenced running to its junction with the B&M at Talyllyn on 1 September 1864. The HH&B completed its final section from Hay to Three Cocks in September 1864 and through running from Hereford to Brecon was instituted on 19 September.

In settlement for their concern the Hay Railway shareholders received 772 shares in the HH&B valued at £9,320 plus £1,881 8s 8d in cash, a total of 11,201 8s 8d.[134]

CHAPTER SEVEN

THE HAY RAILWAY
Finance and Operations

THE preceding chapters have recounted the history of the Hay Railway from its promotion and construction through to its final demise. The present chapter will bring together and summarise what information is available on its financial and operational matters.

Evidence for the financial performance of the company is limited, although accounts survive for the period to 1843, which show a modest level of attainment. So far as operational matters are concerned, most of the information derives from entries in the company records. In the case of the track, archaeological investigation has also brought further evidence to light. It is unfortunate that it is not possible to describe in greater detail the way in which day-to-day activities were carried out on the Hay Railway over its life-span of fifty years.

Financial arrangements

ONLY two copies of annual accounts of the Hay Railway have been seen, those for 1823 and 1843.[135] Both sets are in the same form and set out the initial expenses of construction followed by the totals of annual receipts and expenditure in total, with a shortened form of the current year's trading account. Whilst neither is particularly informative, it is possible to extrapolate figures which give a fair indication of the reasons for the company's lack of financial success.

To deal first of all with the initial receipts, it has been shown above that the authorised capital of £50,000 was not realised, only £42,540 being received. This indicates that there must have been some shares on which not all calls were met. How many, it is not possible to ascertain, but in view of the fact that the Act of 1860, which authorised the purchase of the company by the HH&B, quotes the company's share capital as £42,800, it would appear that some shares were forfeited for non-payment of calls and later taken up by other parties. The amount received from loans was £16,642, an excess of £1,642 above the authorised borrowing. This total can be broken down into £8,000 received on account of the Exchequer Loan, £6,805 from the Hay Railway Optional Loan, and £42 on account of the payment made by promissory note to Thomas Bowen on 23 November 1818 for his land and subsequently taken over by Spencer and treated as a loan to the company. This leaves £1,795 which was probably borrowed from the company's bankers, Wilkins & Co., and covered by the promissory note issued on 22 March 1815.

The costs of construction of the tramroad are shown in TABLE B. The final total is £10,636 5s 4d more than Hodgkinson's estimate for the line through the tunnel. Worse still, the line had cost £3,198 more than the money which the company had to meet the cost – a deficit that dogged its fortunes throughout its existence.

In addition the company had to meet the interest charges on its borrowings. During the currency of the Exchequer Loan the interest would have amounted to £4,200. Whilst the amount paid in interest on account of the Optional Loan seems to have fluctuated as some promissory notes were redeemed and others issued, in 1833 the charges on this account amounted to £327 2s, which indicates that notes to the tune of £6,542 had yet to be redeemed. As by this time the loan had been current for seventeen years the company would have had to pay at least £5,560 to the holders of the notes. By that date the Exchequer Loan had cost the company £4,000 in interest, making a total to that date of £9,560 – no small sum to a company starting life under-capitalised and with a deficit of £4,198 on its construction.

By 1843 the promissory notes had all been redeemed except for £150 and, of course, the Exchequer Loan had been paid off. By that time the total overall profit of the company after 27 years of trading amounted to a mere £713! The fluctuating fortunes of the company can be seen set out in Table D, which can be summarised so far as trading was concerned in Table C.

The average trading receipts from all sources – it is not possible to ascertain how much of this was from tonnages – work out at £2,354. The average expenses, again impossible to itemise, come to £2,172 over the 27 years covered by the accounts.

Track

THE track of the Hay Railway was laid to a nominal gauge of 3 feet 6 inches. The word 'nominal' is used advisedly, as measurements taken from a tie-bar and plate found at Highgrove, Llanhamlach (SO 09822755) in 1977 indicate that the actual gauge of the rails over the guiding faces of the plates was 3 feet 5 inches, leaving 3 feet 6 inches to be the official distance between the backs of the wheels.[136] This would be in accordance with two other local tramroads for which measurements have been obtained, the Brinore Tramroad[137] and the Hereford Railway,[138] both of which laid their rails in tie-bars. The latter was one of Hodgkinson's concerns. As far as the Hay Railway was concerned, it is thought that only the section through Talyllyn tunnel was laid in this manner under a committee resolution of 8 August 1820.

The form of tie-bar used by the Hay Railway necessitated a special form of plate.[139] The tie-bars were cast with holes in the chair portion of the bar and were apparently fixed to the stone blocks. It is

TABLE B: Costs of construction of the Hay Railway.

Legal expenses (these would have included Parliamentary legal fees and conveyancing of the land used)	£3,089	9s	5d
Engineering	2,754	4	6d
Land	9,552	2	8d
Tramplates	17,099	18	10d
Works (contracting)	30,884	7	11d
TOTAL	£63,380	3s	4d

TABLE C: Hay Railway summary trading account, 1811–43.

Receipts from all sources	£122,747		Total expenses	£122,034
less subscriptions and loans	59,182		less construction	63,380
				58,654
			Profit	4,911
	£63,565			£63,565
Profit	4,911			
less deficit on construction	4,198			
Net profit	£713			

TABLE D: Financial performance of the Hay Railway.

ACCOUNTING PERIOD	RECEIPTS PER ANNUM (£)	ACCUMULATED RECEIPTS (£)	PROFIT OR LOSS TO DATE (£)	EXPENDITURE PER ANNUM (£)	ACCUMULATED EXPENDITURE(£)	PROFIT OR LOSS FOR YEAR(£)
1811–23	78,034		-633	78,667		
1824–30	18,025	96,059	+121	17,271	95,938	+754
1831	2,664	98,723	+18	2,767	98,705	-103
1832	2,258	100,981	+575	1,701	100,406	+557
1833	2,009	102,990	+952	1,632	102,038	+377
1834	2,051	105,041	+332	2,671	104,709	-620
1835	1,973	107,014	+247	2,058	107,767	-85
1836	1,921	108,935	+593	1,575	108,342	+346
1837	2,026	110,961	+265	2,354	110,696	-328
1838	1,914	112,875	+196	1,983	112,679	-69
1839	2,084	114,959	+87	2,193	114,872	-109
1840	1,913	116,872	-4	2,004	116,876	-91
1841	2,026	118,898	+269	1,753	118,629	+273
1842	1,620	120,518	-19	1,908	120,537	-288
1843	2,229	122,747	+713	1,497	122,034	+732

not known if the same spike was used to hold down both bar and rail, or if the bar was fixed separately and the plates wedged into the bars. In the case of the Hereford Railway it appears that the tie-bar was just rested at each end on a block.[140] On the Hay Railway the plates used in conjunction with the tie-bars had notches in their ends to enable them to be laid end-to-end with the more normal plate. It is possible that on the Hay Railway the section through the tunnel was difficult to keep to gauge owing to the movement of the ground. There is evidence for this in the payments authorised on 10 October 1817 for 'raising the tunnel' and on 15 December of the same year for 'cleansing the rocks from the sides and top of the tunnel and raising the height thereof'. Tying the blocks together with the tie-bars would be a means of ensuring that the gauge was maintained.

The remainder of the line appears to have been laid with the more usual type of plate with spikes through notches in the ends of adjacent plates to fix them into the stone blocks. Writing in 1937, F. B. Ellison [141] states that he had found

chairs through which the spikes holding down the plates had been driven; but whilst it is known that this method was employed on the neighbouring Kington Railway, no examples have been found on the Hay Railway by the present writer.

Where the tramroad crossed Whitney bridge double-flanged, or channel, plates, 2 feet long, were used. As these had of necessity to be laid parallel with the roadway there must have been considerable inconvenience to the more normal vehicular traffic over the bridge!

The 1811 Act laid down that where the tramroad crossed any turnpike road or highway 'the Ledge or Flanche of such Railway' should not 'exceed One Inch in Height above the level of such Road'. Plates found at Highgrove, where the line crossed a road which formerly linked two farms, show that this proviso was met by the use of special plates, the flange of which was only one inch above the tread and which could consequently be laid with the tread level with the road. That this was the company's standard policy is confirmed by a plate found at Whitney.[142]

E.W.P.T S '9⁻

4. On the left are shown various Hay Railway track pes. Several types of track were used on the Hay ailway. The commonest form, which was used on nost of the line, consisted of cast-iron plates, about 3 :et long, abutted end to end and fixed to stout stone llocks by means of an iron spike between the djoining ends of the plates. In some cases the plate nds were curved, so that the convex end of one fitted ne concave end of the next. The space between the lates was filled with small stones to pack the blocks ght into place and to provide a firm footing for the orses.

)n some sections of the Hay Railway, and in articular in the Talyllyn tunnel, cast-iron tie bars vere used to ensure that the track was held to gauge. he tie bars, with chairs cast on at either end, were laced on the stone blocks and the plates were then tted into the chairs. The whole ensemble was then xed to the sleeper blocks by means of spikes through oth plates and chair.

Specialised forms of tramplate were used at level crossings, and several different versions are known, in every case the purpose being to reduce the obstruction to road traffic caused by the plates. The simplest version was a plate of the conventional pattern, but with a flange only one inch high rather than the normal three inches. Also used were plates with a scalloped flange (one side only) or with castellated flanges (both sides of the tread). In both cases the intention was to reduce the possibility of lateral slipping by road vehicles as they crossed the tramplates.

Above is shown the Kington Railway track. On the Kington Railway conventional tramplates were used, but they were fitted into chairs which were then spiked to the sleeper blocks. It is believed that this type of track was also used on some sections of the Hay Railway.

Drawings: Edward Paget-Tomlinson

35. Fragment of a Hay Railway tramplate of the type
used at road crossings, but with castellated rather than scalloped flanges.
Photo: Tim Edmonds, by permission of Hereford City Museums (1993)

36. Two fragments of trackwork retrieved from the Hay and Kington Railways.
On the left is a chair from the Kington Railway, found near Almeley. The piece on the right is part of a scalloped-
edge tramplate used by the Hay Railway at some road crossings. This example was found at the *Boat Inn*, Whitney.
Photo: R. A. Cook (1979)

37. Tramplates found *in situ* at an occupation crossing between Highgrove and
Slade Farm, Llanfihangel Talyllyn. Note the use of tramplates of differing flange height.
Plates with the shallower flange were specifically intended for use on road crossings.
Photo: P. G. Rattenbury (1977)

Traffic

THE whole line was single-tracked with passing places. No standard distance between passing places seems to have been laid down, but they were probably placed at quarter-mile or one-third mile intervals at places where there was mutual visibility for traffic in either direction. A committee order of 17 September 1829 limited the number of waggons permitted in any one train to eight, which gives an indication of the length of the passing places, as the order was doubtless imposed to ensure that the whole train and its horses could be accommodated clear of the running line. A train of this length would have needed at least three horses and without detaching them it would have measured about 35–40 yards long, which would mean that the passing places were approximately two chains in length between the partings at either end.

Bye-law XIV laid down that traffic going towards Eardisley should have precedence over that towards Brecon, which indicates that as early as 1816, when the bye-laws were formulated, it was realised that downward traffic was likely to consist of empty waggons returning to Brecon. It is not known what means was adopted to regulate traffic through the Talyllyn tunnel – possibly it was some primitive form of token carried in alternate directions by the hauliers, as was the practice on the Bullo Pill Railway to regulate the Haie tunnel.[143]

Brecknock & Abergavenny, Canal Company's Wharf.

JOSEPH DUNN's COAL BY RAIL-WAY, *17th March* 183*4*

Proprietors of Trams.	Hauliers Names.	No. of Trams.	Tare Weight	Gross Weight	Nett Weight

Wm Bridgwater — *Richd Richard* — 148, 159, 151, 131, 184, 151; *Wm Lloyd* — 196. *Jas James Machine Clerk.*

BRECKNOCK BOAT COMPANY'S WHARF.

COAL BY HAY RAILWAY. *6 Feby* 18*52*

Proprietors of Trams	Haulier's Names.	No. of Tram.	Tare Weight			Gross Weight			Nett Weight.		
			Tons	cwts	qrs.	Tons	cwts	qrs.	Tons	cwts	qrs.
Wm Bridgwater	*Wm Lloyd*	101	1	2	2	4	2	2	3	0	
		102	1	3	1	4	3	1	3	0	
									6	0	

Morgan, Printer, Brecon.)

38. Examples of the way bills referred to in the text.
Note the greater capacity of waggons 101 and 102 as compared to the others.
William Bridgwater of Llwynau Bach, Glasbury was one of the major traders on both railways.
By permission of Hereford & Worcester County Record Office (Hereford)

The times at which the tramroad was operative varied according to the time of the year:

November to February	6 am to 6 pm
March, April, September, October	5 am to 8 pm
May to August	4 am to 9 pm

A resolution of 15 December 1817 permitted traffic rated at 4½d per ton per mile to be carried at any hour of the day or night. It cannot be ascertained what traffic was affected by this ruling as this particular rate does not appear in any published account that has been found. There remains the possibility that this was a special rate charged on traffic wishing to pass out of hours. Under bye-law XXI no traffic was permitted on 'Sundays, Christmas Day, Good Friday or any other day of Public Fast or Thanksgiving', and all of the company's wharves were closed on these days.

A series of way-bills covering traffic leaving Brecon between Wednesday 1 February and Saturday 24 March 1832 has survived.[144] They show that in this 53-day period (42 working days) 639 tons of coal, 103 tons of lime and 18 tons of miscellaneous goods were carried – an average of 18 tons 1¾ hundredweight per day. These quantities would have required twelve waggons each with a capacity of 1½ tons. Even assuming that all loads were carried the full distance from Brecon to Eardisley (which may by no means have been the case), tonnages arising from this quantity would have resulted in receipts of £219, the equivalent of £1,662 over a full year. As receipts for the year ended June 1832 amounted to £2,258, either the way-bills do not cover all traffic emanating from Brecon or they coincide with a slack period. A summary of the traffic concerned is shown in TABLE E.[145]

All waggons had to bear the name of the owner, and within three days of being put on the rails they were to be weighed by the company and the tare weight painted on the side. Each waggon had to be numbered, but it is not clear if the number was allocated by the owner or by the company. The highest number of a waggon recorded on the way-bills was 220, but as only 130 are recorded as having been loaded a number of them must probably have fallen out of use during the sixteen years since the opening of the tramroad. The waggons varied in tare weight from 8 hundredweight 2 quarters to 12 hundredweight, and their capacities from 1½ to 1¾ tons. There were four heavier waggons (nos 101–104) in use in the period concerned. These weighed between 1 ton 3 cwt and 2 tons 2 cwt and carried between 2½ and 3 tons load. They were probably the 'double trams' referred to in connection with the purchase of the weighing-machines, but it is not known if they were mounted on bogeys or if the track was expected to bear the extra weight on four wheels only.[146] From the frequency with which most waggons appeared at Brecon for loading it would seem that the 24 miles from Brecon to Eardisley were normally covered in a day. On 4 February 1832 one haulier took two trains out and possibly the trains were handed over at Talgarth to other hauliers for the completion of the journey, the original horses being used to return empty waggons to Brecon.

Coke and lime were both carried in barrels which weighed, nominally, 2 hundredweight 14 pounds and 2½ hundredweight respectively, fourteen barrels of either being the maximum load permitted.

TABLE E: Cargoes loaded at Brecon from 1 February to 24 March 1832.[147]

	TONS	CWT	QRS
Overton & Co's coal	142	0	0
Brecknock Boat Co's wharf			
coal	132	12	2
coke	7	10	0
pig iron	5	0	0
brick	3	0	0
goods	2	7	0
Overton & Scroop's coal	193	13	0
Joseph Dunn's coal	171	3	1
Overton & Co's lime	102	13	0
Total coal	639	8	3
Total lime	102	13	0
Miscellaneous	17	17	0
Grand total	759	18	3

Kington Railway Tram

Found at Dolyhir, September 1963

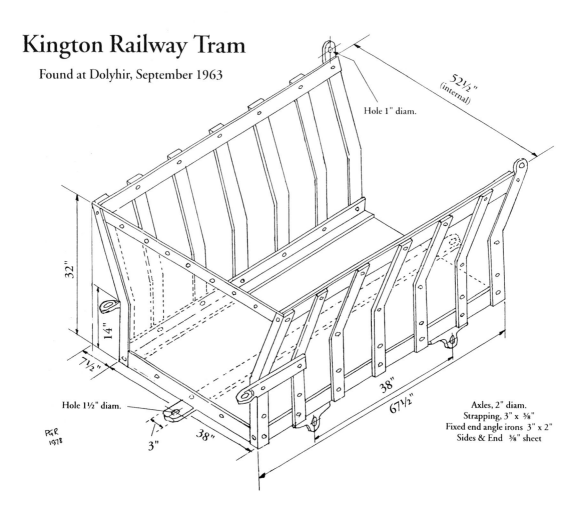

Hole 1" diam.

52½ "
(internal)

32"

14"

7½ "

Hole 1½" diam.

PGR
1978

3"

38"

38"

67½"

Axles, 2" diam.
Strapping, 3" x ⅜"
Fixed end angle irons 3" x 2"
Sides & End ⅜" sheet

39. Drawing of Kington Railway tram, found at Dolyhir.
Drawing: P. G. Rattenbury

76

40. Remains of a Kington Railway tram found at Dolyhir quarry.
This is perhaps the same tram as the one which was photographed by F. B. Ellison on the side of the Kington to New Radnor road near Stanner Rocks (*Transactions of the Woolhope Naturalists Field Club*, 1936–7–8, facing p.81)
Photo: P. G. Rattenbury (1963)

Waggons

THE waggons used on the Hay Railway were probably the motley collection usual on tramroads, each being built to its owner's design, either in wood or iron, the tramroad company being interested only so far as the gauge of the wheels was concerned. In 1963 the remains of an iron waggon were unearthed at Dolyhir, on the Kington Railway (SO 242582). George Overton is known to have owned kilns and quarries at Dolyhir and to have carried coal there from Brecon, also to have been a strong proponent of iron waggons.[148] Whilst no proof is forthcoming, there is a likelihood that this belonged to him or to one of his successors in the quarries. Measurements taken at the time show that it was 67½ inches long and 38 inches wide at floor level, with

77

41. Part of a waggon wheel, now preserved in Hereford City Museum and stated to be from the Hay Railway.
The initial 'T' may be that of Benjamin Trusted of Hay, a haulage contractor on the railway.
Photo: Tim Edmonds, by permission of Hereford City Museums (1993)

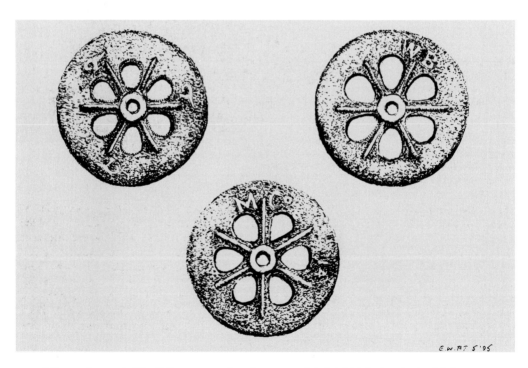

42. Many traders on the Hay Railway seem to have incorporated their initials in the wheels of their waggons.
Known examples include 'W B' (William Bridgwater), 'M Co' (Meredith & Co),
and 'T' (possibly Benjamin Trusted).
Drawing: Edward Paget-Tomlinson

43. Wheel and short length of tramplate recovered from the river Wye in 1975 and now preserved in Hay public library. The wheel has been stated to be from a tramroad waggon, although it is completely different in style to any other known example from the Hay Railway.
Photo: Tim Edmonds (1993)

the sides flared at 14 inches above the floor to open out to a maximum width of 52½ inches at a height of 32 inches. One end was hinged to open upwards, but the end panel was missing. A bar, 3 inches by 1 inch, under the floor extended 6 inches beyond the body at either end to provide a drawbar. Rings to provide attachment for the traces were fitted at 14 inches above the floor level, and could doubtless have been used to attach the shafts which were ordered to be used on the leading waggon by a committee order of 17 September 1829. The axle-trees were 38 inches apart, complying with company regulations.

There does not seem to have been any regulation on the Hay Railway in respect of the width of wheel rims. In guiding the waggons the flange of the plates tended to grind the rims of the wheels to a knife-edge, which in extreme cases could actually cut through the tread of the plate. Whilst the remains of the plates that have been found on the Hay Railway give no evidence of this having been one of the company's problems, it was no doubt one of the difficulties with which the company had to contend in keeping the line in order.

The gradients of the Hay Railway were very moderate by tramroad standards, and the regulation usually found forbidding the use of sprags to lock the waggon wheels does not feature in the company's bye-laws.

44. The Kington Railway passed close by the *Tram Inn* at Eardisley.
The modern inn sign shows an artist's representation of the railway.
Drawing: Edward Paget-Tomlinson

CHAPTER EIGHT

The Kington Railway

(1818 – 1875)

In the closing years of the eighteenth century there were several schemes to provide transport to the small market town of Kington on the Herefordshire/Radnorshire border. In January 1790 a canal was proposed from Stourport on Severn to Leominster, and the following April a meeting in Kington proposed that it should be extended to that town with a view to making Staffordshire coal available there. In the event the canal that resulted ran only from Leominster to Mamble, Worcestershire, where there were small coal mines, and this was the only source of coal to be made available. The extension to Kington was not made, neither was a tramroad over the full route which was proposed by John Hodgkinson in 1803, in spite of its being included in an Act obtained by the canal company in August 1803.[149]

The inadequate state of transport in the whole district is brought out in a paragraph which appeared in *The Cambrian* of 19 January 1805, reporting that eight parishes on the road from Brecon to Hay had been indicted at the Brecon Quarter Sessions for failure to maintain their roads, 'the road in some places being impassable'. Six years later the preamble to the Act for the Hay Railway from Brecon to Parton Cross (SO 313482) stated that owing to the poor state of the roads a railway would be of great public advantage.[150] In the following year, 1812, the Hay Railway obtained a further Act altering parts of its route and changing the northern terminal to Eardisley (SO 313492).[151]

The towns of Hay and Kington, standing some ten miles apart, were of similar size. There is no doubt that once the inhabitants of Kington saw the benefit of cheaper coal which was made possible by the completion of the tramroad to Hay in May 1816, they were led to consider how they could obtain such advantages themselves, bearing in mind particularly the superiority of Monmouthshire coal over that from the Worcestershire source.[152]

Early in 1818, with the Hay Railway under construction from Hay to Eardisley, a prospectus was issued delineating two possible routes for a tramroad which would put Kington on the transport map. The first suggestion was for a line from Whitney on Wye (SO 268474), rising by 510 feet to Bollingham (SO 302527) and then descending in the valley of the River Arrow to Kington, a distance of ten miles, which might be made for an estimated £14,500. The second route would rise 238 feet from the Eardisley terminus of the Hay Railway to Elsdon (SO 321546) and then fall steadily via Lyonshall Park Wood (SO 325567) to Kington, a distance of eight miles to be made for an estimated £11,000. Either line could be extended by four miles to the quarries at Burlinjobb (SO 241581) 'at a trifling gradient' which would cost an additional £5,380.[153] In a letter to Sir Charles Morgan of Tredegar, near Newport, Monmouthshire which was written on the back of a copy of the prospectus, James Davies, of the Kington & Radnorshire Bank,[154] solicited his support for one or other of the schemes and extolled the virtues of tramroads in comparison with canals from the point of view of reliability and expressed his belief that the towns of both Hay and Brecon would benefit from increased supplies of corn should the tramroad be made.

An application for leave to introduce a Bill was made to Parliament early in March 1818, but the necessary preliminary of depositing plans with the Clerks of the Peace for Radnorshire and Herefordshire had been omitted, as had the publication in the papers of both counties of notices of intent. On 18 March the *Hereford Journal* contained a notice stating that a Bill had been deposited for 'a Rail-Way or Tram-Road from the Hay Railway near Eardisley … to the Lime Works near Burlinjobb' and that on 12 March the House had ordered the deposit of plans and books of reference with the proper authorities; also that the tramroad was intended to pass through the parishes of Eardisley, Spond, Lyonshall, Kington, Lower Burlinjobb and Old Radnor. A similar notice appeared in the issue of 8 April stating that plans of the parts of the line affecting the various parishes would be deposited with the various Clerks on 15 April. Once this had been done, Parliament acted with amazing celerity and the

Act for the Kington Railway received the Royal Assent on 23 May 1818 (58 Geo. III c.63).

The financial clauses of the Act were somewhat unusual. The authorised capital was stated to be £18,000 in shares of £100 each, with powers to borrow a further £5,000. The promoters named in the Bill had only subscribed £11,900, however, by the time they went to Parliament and while it was in the House a further £1,500 was promised, making a total of £13,400. The estimated cost of the line was stated to be £16,444, and the Act stipulated that work was not to commence until £16,000 had become available. A list of subscribers, written on a loose sheet of paper and fixed in the minute book, shows that further £2,400 had been promised by the time of the inaugural meeting, which was held on 2 June 1818, making a total of £15,800.[155] It was, however, decided to proceed with the plan. A list of subscribers is given in APPENDIX B. Clause 42 of the Act authorised the raising of capital by the issue of promissory notes, but gives no indication of what security was to be offered as a guarantee of repayment.

45. Kington Railway waggon plate, now preserved in Hereford City Museum.
Regulations required the name of the owner and the number of the waggon to be shown on each waggon.
'I & J W Meredith' must indicate the brothers John and James Woodhouse Meredith who operated Kington Foundry after their father's death in 1823. Since James Woodhouse Meredith himself died in 1826, this plate can therefore be dated to 1823–6. If this interpretation is correct, it is strange that the Latinate 'I' should have been used as John's initial whilst James used a 'J'.
Photo: Tim Edmonds, by permission of Hereford City Museums (1993)

46. Complete length of tramplate from the Kington Railway,
found near Eardisley and now preserved in the *Tram Inn*, Eardisley.
Photo: Stephen K. Jones (1994) by permission of Ms C. Reynolds

The remaining terms of the Act were more usual. The rails were not to stand above the level of any road crossed by more than one inch. The hours during which the tramroad might be used were laid down as:

November to February	7 am to 5 pm
March, April, September, October	6 am to 8 pm
May to August	6 am to 9 pm

Owners' names were to be shown on the sides of the waggons in letters one inch high, and the penalties for mis-use of the tramroad included transportation for seven years for removal of any part of the track. Any owner of land adjoining the tramroad might make a branch into it, and should the company refuse to make a wharf on his land, he was to be at liberty to make it for himself. Should the company fail to fence the tramroad the landowner was free to do it himself at the cost of the company. The Act stipulated the maximum tonnages (i.e. charges) that might be made for the use of the tramroad and allowed the unusually long time of ten years for its completion.

At the inaugural meeting doubts were expressed as to the likelihood of the Hay Railway completing its line to Eardisley, whence it was expected that the greatest part of the Kington Railway's trade would originate, and whether that company had yet decided on the manner of crossing the river Wye at Whitney. Six shareholders were appointed as a deputation to attend a meeting of the Hay Railway to ascertain whether

it would be worth while to proceed: subject to a satisfactory report it was decided to start construction as soon as possible. Advertisements were to be placed in the Herefordshire, Swansea, Shrewsbury and Gloucester papers asking prospective contractors to submit tenders before 26 June. The advertisement in the *Hereford Journal* of 10 July 1818, signed by Davies & Banks, the company's solicitors, stated that only one contractor would be appointed for the whole twelve miles from Eardisley to Burlinjobb, and that he would be expected to keep the line in repair for ten years after completion. It was normal for contracts for tramroad construction to state that stone blocks and rails would be supplied by the company, but in the case of the Kington Railway

... it is intended that every expence, except the price of land, shall be comprehended in the contract, and it will be required that ample security shall be given for the performance of such contract.

The provision of one contractor only was probably an indication that note had been taken of the experience of the Hay Railway with its numerous failures of contractor.

Two tenders were read at a meeting on 13 July, one from William Hazledine (a Shrewsbury ironfounder) and Morris Sayce (surveyor, of Kington), and the other from John Hodgkinson, who was under contract at the time to complete the Hay Railway to Eardisley, but no decision was taken. By the next meeting, on 18 July, a further tender had been received from George Overton, the engineer of the Merthyr Tramroad, and all three were considered. That of Hodgkinson was rejected out of hand as it was not thought to be in line with the terms of the advertisement and Davies & Banks were instructed to inform him of this. Possibly in the hope of receiving further offers, a decision was again deferred for a week. Meeting on 25 July, the proprietors had a tender from Benjamin Ball (of whom no details have been found) to consider in addition to those of Hazledine & Sayce and Overton. It was decided to award the contract to Hazledine & Sayce in the sum of £14,000, and the chairman was authorised to sign the contract as soon as it had been prepared.

Davies reported to the meeting on 25 July that he had received a letter from James Spencer, the Clerk to the Hay Railway, inviting the deputation appointed on 2 June to attend his company's meeting on 28 July. The deputation reported to the Kington Railway meeting on 5 September that

47. Initials 'E V' on the tread of the Kington Railway plate preserved at Eardisley. The most obvious interpretation of these is 'Ebbw Vale', i.e. the ironworks where the plate was manufactured. However, F. B. Ellison prefers to interpret the initials as those of Evan Vaughan of Clydach. Photo: Stephen K. Jones (1994) by permission of Ms C. Reynolds

they were satisfied that the Hay Railway would shortly be completed, and Sayce was instructed to lay out the line and to survey and value the land as he proceeded, the intention being that when this was completed the committee would start negotiations with the landowners. The meeting ordered a call of 10 per cent due on 9 October, for which date a meeting was called to appoint a Treasurer and Clerk to the company.

On 18 September Hazledine & Sayce reported that it was essential that they should know the exact level of the Hay Railway terminus at Eardisley, and Davies & Banks were instructed to apply to the Hay company for their contractor – Hodgkinson – to supply the necessary information. The contractors were reminded that it would be necessary for them to submit the names of their sureties before 29 September in order that the contract might be signed at the meeting on 9 October.

At the September meeting it was revealed that Sayce was not satisfied with the Parliamentary line where it passed through the land of J. Lloyd Harris of the Moor (now known as Lynhales) (SO 325552) and that of John Cheese at Lyonshall Park (SO 323573). Anxious not to tread on the toes of either gentleman, both of whom were shareholders, the meeting ordered that Sayce should make no alterations to the plan 'without ascertaining that such deviations will be for the general good of the concern or at least equally so', and that he should forthwith make an accurate survey in the presence of both Harris and Cheese, which survey would show the exact rate of fall from Elsdon to Kington. He was also to do a similar job on the whole route, and was reminded that his sureties would be expected to stand for the maintenance portion of the contract as well as for the initial construction.

Sayce had his proposals ready for approval at the meeting on 17 October 1818. These involved carrying the line further to the west at Lyonshall thereby avoiding several of Cheese's fields, but taking it closer to the Moor than was shown on Hodgkinson's plans. Whilst this involved a slight increase in the summit level, he would be able to even out the gradient by modest earthworks. Similar adjustments were proposed between Eardisley and Upcott, and thence to Elsdon. The

48. Kington Railway cutting at Elsdon, looking south-east towards Eardisley.
The cutting had already started to be used as a refuse dump when this photograph was taken.
The process has continued and the cutting is now completely full, although the parapets of the bridge
and the crown of the arch are still visible.
Photo: R. A. Cook (1958)

meeting resolved to purchase a spirit-level and a steelyard for the use of the company, and on a proposal by James Watt, the pioneer steam engineer who had retired to the district, it was decided to increase both the thickness and the breadth of the 'shoes' (i.e. chairs), the company to pay for the additional weight of iron required. Sayce was instructed to start work as soon as the contract had been signed.

The meeting went on to elect James Davies, of the Kington & Radnorshire Bank, as Treasurer, and John C. Cheese (not the landowner – the Cheese family was most numerous in the district) as Clerk. It was also decided to appoint an engineer to examine the manner in which Hazledine & Sayce were performing their contract from time to time as the committee might require.

On 30 December 1818 the *Hereford Journal* reported that construction had been in progress for some weeks and that it was believed that it would be completed 'as rapidly as the nature of the undertaking will permit'. The Hay Railway had already, on 23 November, contracted with John Hodgkinson in the sum of £150 to construct a connecting line to meet the Kington Railway, the Hay Railway to provide land and plates.[156] The minutes of neither company reveal why this was undertaken by the Hay Railway, and the Kington Railway's plans show that their line was to terminate on the eastern edge of the Hereford–Kington road (the present A4111) with only the actual road crossing to be made. Working proportionally on the cost of similar work on the Hay Railway, Hodgkinson was paid for approximately

150 yards of track-bed.[157] This would place the terminus of the Kington Railway at approximately so 31404905. The extension remained the property of the Hay Railway, and this is shown by a request by the Kington Railway to the Hereford, Hay & Brecon Railway (who purchased the Hay Railway in 1860) that they might continue to use the extension to reach the erstwhile Hay company's wharf at Eardisley.[158]

The Hereford paper of 16 June 1819 reported that the line was progressing rapidly, 'which must afford great pleasure to all whose interest is connected with so beneficial an undertaking. On 26 October 'Messrs. Sayce' were paid £1,000 on account of their contract work.

The contract required that the tramroad should be completed by 1 April 1820, and on 1 March the committee resolved that it should be opened for traffic from Eardisley to the Floodgates, Kington (so 28825704) on 1 May.

On 17 April the general meeting ordered that the bye-laws governing the use of the tramroad and the list of tonnages to be charged, which had been agreed at the meeting, should be printed for distribution. In ordering the company's common seal, the Clerk was instructed to ensure that it was delivered with a 'screw-engine', but if possible it should be capable of use without the 'engine'. The

site of the company's main wharf at Sunset, Kington was apparently in an advanced state and it was ordered that stone walls should be built on the south-west and south-east sides leaving 'proper apertures' for gates. The Clerk was instructed to consult with Spencer, the Clerk to the Hay Railway, for suggestions for suitable persons to act as toll-clerks.

The traders, too, made their preparations for the opening, to judge by an advertisement inserted in the *Hereford Journal* of 26 April by 'Sayce & Cheese' to the effect that as from 1 May there would be a constant supply of household and lime-burning coals at Kington and Lyonshall wharves, 'and as the prices are intended to be moderate the public are respectfully informed that payment will be expected on delivery'. The advertisement does not quote the initials of either partner and it is impossible to ascertain if either was associated with the tramroad.

The final call of £15 per share was made on 18 March to be paid by 20 April.[159] The response to the calls was probably disappointing, as on 31 October it was resolved that 'the money wanting to complete the undertaking had better be raised by allowing the present subscribers to increase their number of shares in preference to borrowing', but with a rider that should insufficient

49. The drive leading to Lynhales (formerly The Moor) follows the line of the Kington Railway. Lyonshall wharf was established at this point where the tramroad crossed the turnpike road, now the A44 between Kington and Leominster. Photo: Stephen K. Jones (1994)

50. The Kington Railway passes Eardisley on a long low embankment to the east of the village.
A train trundles over a small culvert through this embankment on its way to Kington.
Drawing: Edward Paget-Tomlinson

money be forthcoming within a fortnight loans should be sought 'on the credit of the railway'. It was ordered that the weighing-machine which had been procured should be erected 'near the entrance on the railway at Eardisley with a sentry-box', and instructions were given for the erection of boards giving the substance of the bye-laws in respect of 'passing, riding or driving cattle on the railway'. Sayce was instructed to submit his claim for interest on money expended to the scrutiny of three members, while his suggestions for a revision of the maintenance terms of his contract were deferred until the next committee meeting.

The tramroad was completed to Burlinjobb and opened throughout on Monday 7 August 1820.[160]

Complaints were received at the general meeting on 19 July 1821 from John Sherbourne and James Watt, junior – his father had died in 1819 – that the line had not yet been fenced where it passed through their lands. The Clerk was instructed to write to Sayce ordering him to fence the land concerned with hurdles 'until the season arrive for properly planting the same with quicksetts' (i.e. hawthorns). Watt had not yet been paid for his land and the Treasurer was ordered to pay him £33 8s 3d straightaway. There were also complaints that many parts of the tramroad were impassable and that permanent bridges had not been erected over the river Arrow at SO 30685694 and the Back brook at SO 29035697: a resolution was passed …

… that the contractors be peremptorily required to complete the whole of the Road in every particular in fulfilment of their contract within two months.

There were also two claims for damages done to property while construction had been in progress. One was from W. Symonds, the owner of Elsdon Quarry, which it was decided should be settled by each party appointing an assessor; the other was from E. B. Pateshall, of Allensmore, near Hereford, in respect of rubbish that had been thrown on his land at Lyonshall. The Clerk was instructed to write to him stating that unless he wished to claim the land and accept £10 damages it was the company's intention to purchase the land under the compulsory purchase powers granted in their Act. He was given fourteen days to appeal against the decision. Finally, the meeting voted to pay the Clerk £80 in respect of his salary to the previous October, 'being the yearly sum of £50'.

The suggestion made on 31 October 1820 that proprietors might increase the number of shares which they held had not met with a ready response, as was revealed on 13 October 1821 by a resolution that interest on mortgages should be paid as it fell due. The amounts that had been borrowed are not stated in the minutes.

The meeting considered a letter that had been received from George Overton, who had a large interest in the quarries and kilns at Dolyhir, asking for a 'drawback'(i.e. rebate) to be granted on the coal he was using to burn lime, a concession that the Hay Railway had withdrawn in August 1820. It was decided that the solicitors should confer with John Powell of the BBCO., the Brecon whole-

51 *(left)*. The bridge near Gipsy Hall, between Eardisley and Upcott, which carried the Kington Railway over
Holywell Dingle, as it might have been when the Kington Railway was operational and, 52 *(right)*, as it is now.
Drawing: Edward Paget-Tomlinson. Photo: Stephen K. Jones (1994)

salers of coal, before a decision was made. The
proprietors expressed doubt as to the quality of
Sayce's work at this meeting, and the committee
were instructed to

… perambulate the whole line of the Road
particularly with a view to the subject of the
covering the blocks with gravel, and form their
opinion within three weeks.

The result of their inspection is not known, due to
the absence of the committee minutes, which do
not appear to have survived.

Advantage was taken of the advent of the
tramroad in September 1821, when two local
Justices of the Peace gave notice of a motion to
be submitted to the next Quarter Sessions in
Hereford to alter the 'footway' from Gipsy Hall

(SO 31755016) to Almeley so as to run alongside the
tramroad via Upcott bridge (SO 32675088) to the
point where it crossed the Almeley to Nieuport
road at SO 32905162, thus putting the road on the
line which it now occupies.[161]

From October 1821 the Kington Railway
changed its practice of holding several general
meetings each year and thereafter held only the
one annual meeting in October, the day-to-day
running of the company being left to the committee. One result of this was that only routine
information appears in the minutes, and the
intimate details of the company are not recorded.
One matter which did come to the attention of
the proprietors was when, at their meeting on 29
October 1822, James Watkins, a chandler, was
called upon to explain why he had built a wall on

the company's land at Crooked Well, Kington (so 295969) which enclosed part of their property. He was allowed to leave the wall and to retain the land on which it was built on payment of 7s per annum rent provided that he also maintained the company's wall on the other side of the tramroad. There was evidently a passing place here, as he was to look after the company's wall 'as far as the turnout extends'. Also present at this meeting was Thomas Meredith, of the Kington Foundry, who claimed that construction of the tramroad had interfered with the water supply to his works and had damaged some of his trees, one of which he valued at £2 5s. The company offered to settle the matter by arbitration but he would not agree, whereupon he was offered compensation of £6 in settlement, and the Clerk actually tendered six sovereigns which Meredith refused to pick up from the table. It is not known how this dispute ended.

It was realised in 1823 that, whilst the company had decided on its regulations before the tramroad was actually opened, there was no record in the minute book of the terms, and the meeting of 28 October had them set out *in extenso,* occupying several folios of the book. In substance these were similar to those of the Hay Railway but with local variations such as the erecting of a post mid-way between passing places. Also, whilst unladen waggons were to give way to those with a load, where two trains of equal status were involved, the one arriving first at the post had right of way and the other was to pull back to the previous passing place. The maximum weight permitted was limited to two tons per waggon, to include the weight of the waggon. The Hay Railway permitted the combined weights to be 2½ tons, which must have caused a certain amount of difficulty where through traffic was concerned.[162]

Meeting on 26 October 1824 the proprietors considered a request from Meredith for an alteration to the turnout into his works to the east of Kington (so 302569), and three committee members were authorised to effect the required alterations, should they think fit. The meeting voted the sum of £82 2s to be paid to Davies & Banks, their fees for conveyancing.

There was considerable dissatisfaction with the maintenance work of Hazledine & Sayce and in 1825 the general meeting decided to pay them the £36 owing to the end of 1824 less such sum as might be judged to be due from them for failure

53. Line of the Kington Railway at Crooked Well on the western outskirts of Kington. Note how the end wall of the house has been built at an acute angle in order to fit a site which had already been defined by the tramroad. Photo: Stephen K. Jones (1994)

54. Meredith's foundry, Kington. The foundry was erected by John Meredith in about 1820 on a site alongside the then newly constructed tramroad, which was to be the means of supplying it with coal and iron. On his death in 1823 the foundry passed to his two sons, John Meredith II and James Woodhouse Meredith. In later years the building was used as a laundry and now houses a number of small workshops.
Photo: R. A. Cook (1958)

to abide by the terms of their contract. Nor were the proprietors too happy with the toll-clerk at Eardisley, one West, who was ordered to present himself at the next committee meeting

… to learn from him his time and manner of attending to the duties of his office with a view to improvement in his department.

It is possible that he had some side-line, as the following item in the minutes is an instruction to the Clerk to advertise for a toll-clerk for Sunset wharf, Kington, 'who will exclusively be the servant of the company'.

The Kington & Radnorshire Bank did not escape the difficulties that afflicted banking houses all over the country at the end of 1825, and the *Hereford Journal* of 21 December reported two meetings held in Kington during the previous week at which resolutions had been passed expressing the willingness of the committee to continue to accept locally issued bank-notes. A week later the paper carried an advertisement over the signatures of twelve local lime traders requesting that their customers should continue to pay their bills in notes drawn on the bank 'and other respectable houses, and that in preference to gold or Bank of England paper'. A very strong case of local loyalty!

George Overton died on 2 February 1827,[163] and on 24 October an advertisement appeared in the *Hereford Journal* offering the lease of the kilns at Dolyhir which were stated to be capable of producing 100,000 bushels of lime annually, for which there was a ready market. All enquiries

55 *(above)*. The limekilns at Dolyhir survive on the edge of the modern quarries which are still in active production – many additional structures have been erected in the area; and, 56 *(right)*, as they might have appeared when the Kington Railway was operational. The kilns formed the northern end of the railway and were one of its major sources of traffic. The artist is facing in the direction of Kington.
Photo: Stephen K. Jones (1994). Drawing: Edward Paget-Tomlinson

were to be addressed to 'Messrs. Sayce, Land Surveyors, Kington'.

Even by the standards of the time, the wages paid by the company were low. On 30 October 1827 the Treasurer was instructed to pay Cheese the sum of £18 0s 6d in respect of the toll-clerks' wages for the year. As far as is known, there were only two – one at Eardisley and one at Kington – who would certainly not have been overworked, and this explains why West might well have needed an additional source of income. Cheese was instructed to obtain plans and estimates for 'an improved toll-house' at Eardisley, but the cost was not to exceed £30. He was also to engage a person to keep a check on trams passing Stanner (SO 261582) in order to avoid loss of tonnages, but the sum set aside for this purpose was not to be greater than one guinea annually! Cheese was also instructed to make it public that the weighing-machine at Sunset wharf could be used by the

public at a charge of 3d per cart-load and 6d per waggon-load, and that certificates of weight would be issued. Three committee members were detailed to check the accuracy of the machine.

The meeting on 28 October 1828 emphasised the difficulty that was experienced in obtaining payment of calls by passing a resolution that £25 should be paid to the executors of John Cheese of Castlefaen, an original promoter of the line, in respect of damages done to his property during construction, and that a demand should be made to the executors to pay the sum of £50 in respect of unpaid calls on his five shares.

The principal articles carried by the tramroad were lime, limestone and coal, for which the Act prescribed tonnages of 5d, 3d and 5d respectively per ton per mile. These rates were charged until June 1829 when a special general meeting agreed to the introduction of drawbacks, or rebates, per ton per mile of 3¼d on lime, 1¼d on limestone,

2½d on coal used for lime burning, and 2d on all other coal, making the effective rates per ton per mile:

lime and limestone	1¾d
lime-burning coal	2½d
all other coal	3d

These rates were to apply only if no part of the journey took place on a turnpike road. The minutes of the meeting were signed by all members present, including 'For the late John Cheese, by his Executors: John Cheese and Joseph Bebb'.

Insufficient shares were represented at the meeting in October 1829 for any business to be transacted, but at the adjourned meeting on 10 November the rates on lime and limestone were further reduced by ¼d per ton per mile. The meeting ordered payment to be made to the Clerk of £75 6s 8d, his bill for the erection of the toll-house at Eardisley and for wages.

The amount borrowed by the company can only be judged by the resolutions that were passed for repayments to be made. On 30 October 1827 the loan of £200 from John Wilson was repaid, and a year later that of £600 from John Matthews. On 26 October 1830 the Treasurer was instructed to repay £500 of the £2,050 lent by John Morris and James Davies of the Kington Bank. As far as can be ascertained this £2,850 was the sum total of the company's borrowing. In October 1831 it was decided that all shares with arrears of calls should be forfeited, and when the first dividend was declared in October 1833 it was stated to be £2 per share on £14,700 *valid* shares, indicating that at least eleven shares had not been fully paid. The cost of the tramroad can only be estimated as £17,750 (£14,700 plus borrowing of £2,850), plus an unspecified amount received for calls on forfeited shares. Five shares were advertised for sale in the *Hereford Journal* of 17 February 1836, but it is not possible to ascertain whether these were forfeitures. The final repayment to Morris & Davies was made on 29 October 1839.

After ordering the forfeiture of partly paid shares, the meeting of 25 October 1831 was adjourned to 12 November when it was decided that a mistake had been made in November 1829 in fixing the tonnage on limestone at 1½d per ton per mile and it was resolved that this rate should apply only to stone intended to be converted into lime and not to that intended to be used for road metalling or for footpaths, which was to revert to the Parliamentary charge of 3d per ton per mile. The meeting was adjourned again to 21 November for discussion of a new contract with Sayce to continue the maintenance clauses of the original contract with Hazledine & Sayce. The latter meeting was again adjourned and it was not until 20 December that the terms of the new contract were agreed and the solicitor ordered to prepare the deed.

The contract with Sayce on his own was signed by him on 24 January 1832 and sealed by the company on 14 February. Sayce's brother John was accepted by the company as his surety for due performance. It was decided to reduce the amount of his portion of the damages that the owners of Elsdon Quarry claimed had been done during construction of the tramroad from £38 19s to £25, the company to pay the remainder.

At a committee meeting on 11 April 1832 it was decided to call a special general meeting of the proprietors to consider a reduction in the tonnages on coal,[164] but at the general meeting held on 12 May it was resolved that any reduction in the current rates of 3d per ton on house coal and 2½d on lime-burning coal should be made dependent on the willingness of the coal traders to sell the best coal at Kington at 25s per ton and that the lime traders should reduce the price of their product by 1d per barrel of 280 pounds. Subject to a suitable undertaking, the company would be prepared to make reductions of 1d per ton per mile on house coal and ½d on lime-coal.

Another special meeting on 20 June learned that the traders had not been prepared to reduce their prices, and the company then suggested that if the price of coal was reduced to 26s per ton at

Kington and reduced by 1d per bushel at Radnor they would be prepared to make a charge of 2d per ton per mile on all coal; otherwise the rates would continue at 3d and 2½d respectively on the two types. There is no record in the minutes of reductions in tonnages or prices having taken place. It is perhaps an indication of the general impecuniosity of the district that coal should be sold in such a small quantity as a bushel.[165]

There were evidently suspicions that not all goods carried on the tramroad were being accounted for, and on 30 December 1832 it was ordered that

… the committee do make means to ascertain from the traders on the Tramroad or by any other means they may devise, how many tons of coal or other produce were carried by them along the Road during the year ended this day in order to discover as far as may be whether the whole has been brought to account.

It is not known if the traders were suspected of dishonesty or the toll-clerks of laxity. The result of the investigation is not recorded in the minutes.

The company was not satisfied with the manner in which Sayce was performing his maintenance contract and on 13 May 1833 a special meeting deputed John Mitchell and John Meredith to inspect the whole tramroad and works on 24 May in the company of Sayce's representatives, James Davies and E. W. Cheese, to determine 'the finishing, completion and sufficiency of the repair and condition of the railway'.

Their report indicated numerous faults in construction:

1. Castle Hill and Waterloo bridges (SO 29035697 and SO 30685694) had not been made to the specified widths, but could be considered satisfactory, subject to additional ironwork and extra piling at Waterloo bridge in order to preserve the weir.

2. A considerable quantity of ballast was required to keep the blocks in place and to provide a suitable path (for the horses).

3. Many gates and posts were 'wholly wanting', some were made of the wrong materials 'according to the spirit of the contract', and others required to be repaired.

57 *(above)*. Waterloo Bridge, used by the Kington Railway to cross the river Arrow on the eastern outskirts of Kington. The photograph shows the bridge before it was rebuilt in 1976. Photo: R. A. Cook (1958)

58 *(left)*. Castle Hill bridge over the Back Brook at Floodgates, Kington. Photo: P. G. Rattenbury (1979)

4. The road was 'crooked or zig-zag' at the Flood-gates, and there were undulations between that point and Stanner, all of which should be corrected.

5. There was a declivity between the road to Nieuport (SO 32655208) and the road to Almeley (SO 32805165), but it was left to the general meeting to decide if this should be re-levelled or not.

6. In many parts the gauge of the rails exceeded 3 feet 5¾ inches, which should be corrected. In several other places the gauge was incorrect but would suffice. (The reference to 3 feet 5¾ inches indicates that the gauge of the line, nominally 3 feet 6 inches, was the back-to-back measurement of the waggon wheels.)

7. There were a number of claims outstanding for the non-provision of fences, and it was thought that these cases should remain the responsibility of Sayce.

The tone of the last remark makes it evident that it was considered that Sayce's contract should be terminated in the opinion of those making the inspection, and their opinion was borne out at the general meeting on 18 June 1833 when the final account between the company and Sayce was agreed as shown in TABLE F.

In the minute book this account is followed by a note: 'This balance was paid by the said Company to Mr. M. Sayce, Treasurer's cheque on Kington Bank July 1833'. It is not known over what period Sayce & Parry's debt had been accumulating, but it would represent tonnage on about 4,000 tons of coal – possibly a better source of income than tramroad contracting.

Maintenance appears to have been handed over to direct labour after the departure of Sayce and the meeting in October 1833 ordered the payment to the Clerk of £46 8s 10d to include 'expences incurred in keeping the Road by Daniel Daniel and his assistants since Mr. Sayce relinquished the care of same'. This meeting declared the first dividend to be paid by the company of £2 per share on 'valid subscriptions of £14,700', payable on application to the Kington Bank on 1 January 1834.

In October 1834 the proprietors ordered that

TABLE F: Final account between Morris Sayce and the Kington Railway, 1833.

Balance of mileage (i.e. maintenance) to 1 May 1830	£148 8s 11		
less already paid	100 0 0		£ 48 8 11
Mileage to 1 May 1831			186 0 0
Mileage to 1 May 1832			186 0 0
Mileage to 1 May 1833			186 0 0
Mileage to 25 May 1833 when review was taken			12 15 0
		Total	£619 3s 11d
per contra			
Cash paid to Mr Sayce on account to 31 October 1832			£150 0 0
Tonnages due from Messrs Sayce & Parry to 31 May 1833			258 3 11
Allowance by Mr Sayce in respect of unfulfilled parts of his contract and agreed by the meeting			110 0 0
			518 3 11
Balance to be paid to Mr Sayce			101 0 0
		Total	£619 3 11

59. The former Kington gasworks, opened in 1830, with tramroad waggons in the foreground. The photograph must date from about 1870 at the latest. The gasworks, which has now been demolished, lay on the opposite side of the Back Brook to Meredith's foundry. By permission of Mrs E. H. T. Ridger and Hereford & Worcester County Record Office (Hereford)

Sayce should be paid £41 11s in respect of 'plates, shoes etc. taken by the Company when he quitted the care of the Railway in 1833', and that this sum should be applied to the credit of Sayce & Parry's tonnage account, 'as herebefore directed by Mr. Sayce'. How beneficial to the company was the change from contract to direct labour is shown by an entry in the minutes instructing the Treasurer to pay the Clerk £158 11s 7d in respect of his

… bill of expences incurred in keeping in repair the Railway from the end of September 1833 to the end of the same in 1834, *this sum to include toll-clerks wages, stationery, advertising etc.* (The italics are the author's.)

The following year Cheese was paid £132 14s for the same purposes – a favourable reduction on the £186 per annum previously paid to Sayce for maintenance alone.

A scheme for a tramroad from Stourport to Kington via Leominster was proposed early in 1834 to supersede the incomplete Leominster Canal. It would probably have been of benefit to the people of Kington in enabling them to obtain Staffordshire coal in competition with that from north Monmouthshire. Favourable meetings were held in Stourport and Leominster in January and February, and in April it was reported that the line had been surveyed from Stourport to Leominster – not a very difficult task as it was intended to use the line of the canal, including those parts actually constructed! Nothing more was heard of the proposal after April. The cost of the whole fifty-mile line was estimated at £105,000 – £2,100 per mile.[166]

A notice published in the *Hereford Journal* of 15 February 1837 called a general meeting of the Kington Railway proprietors for 11 March to consider …

… the best mode of repairing the damage lately done to the archway of the waste water at Upcott Pool, and what party is liable to do such repair, whether the Turnpike Trust, the Tramroad Company or the Newport Family [the Foleys].

The meeting on 11 March was adjourned to 15 March, as Banks, the solicitor, had been unable to prepare a case for Counsel's consideration. It was not until 6 April that the case was prepared and agreed by the company. An advertisement in the paper of 22 November, signed by Cheese, invited tenders for the repairs. The cost was probably apportioned between the three parties, as on 30 October 1838 the Treasurer was ordered to 'pay £10 on account of the proportion of expenses in the repair of the culvert at Upcott Pool'.

John C. Cheese tendered his resignation as Clerk on 30 October 1838 on account of his continuing ill-health. It was accepted by the meeting with 'a strong feeling of regret at the cause thereof', and Thomas Price of the Mill was appointed in his stead at the same salary of £50 per annum. After declaring a dividend of £3 per share, the meeting requested Cheese to continue in service until he had completed the accounts to the end of September, and with the help of a Mr Day had collected all the tonnages due to that time, in order that the company might pay off the final instalment of its loan from Morris & Davies.

It was not until 20 December 1841 that the final two years of Cheese's salary to 30 September 1838 were paid, when his executors received £100. At the same time Parry, the machine clerk at Kington, was paid £18 4s for 21 months' salary – 4s per week!

Price attended a meeting on 2 November 1838 and in accepting the position named James Watkins and Samuel R. Owens as his sureties. He was instructed to assist Cheese and Day in sending out tonnage demands, and his general duties were laid down in detail:

To make out quarterly and deliver all bills to the traders with a letter requesting payment to the Treasurer's account.

To make out a general account half-yearly to 1st. April and 1st. October; to inspect the Road weekly or oftener if necessary to see that the workmen do their duty; pay them once a fortnight by cheque on the Treasurer; take up and book accounts of tonnage; keep watch on machine clerks, and generally take care that the Company is not wronged.

Carefully to study the Act to learn the several duties of Clerk, Committee, Proprietors etc. and the liability of Persons trespassing or defrauding or injuring the Road.

He is also to conform to such further directions as shall from time to time be given by the Committee.

With such a list of duties it was hardly necessary for the minutes to add that he would be expected 'to devote the whole or as much as shall be necessary of his time to the performance of his duties'.

No published or detailed accounts of the company have ben found, but the minutes for 16 April 1839 show the following entry:

Cash balance to the credit of the Company £571 5s 4d	
The amount of assets in the hand and to be received	£1,562 18s 8d
Amount of moneys to be paid including all dividends declared	£1,174 4s 11d
	———
Balance	£388 13s 9d

Later minutes, at approximately yearly intervals, contain a statement in similar form (see APPENDIX C). Whilst they show that the company was solvent, they give no indication of the amounts of tonnages received or of expenses for maintenance. It appears that Cheese's efforts to bring in outstanding tonnages were unsuccessful and the meeting of 16 April 1839 voted that Morris & Davies should be paid only £300 in part repayment of their loan and interest. The meeting concluded by resolving that the tonnage on iron should be reduced by 1d per ton per mile if the Hay company would make a similar reduction. The Hay Railway probably concurred, as a further meeting on 29 October reduced the tonnage on iron to 2d per ton per mile for the following year, after which the position would be reviewed.

The Kington Railway was now entering on the most prosperous period of its existence, and in October 1839 declared the highest dividend which it was ever to attain – £3 10s per share – which was maintained until 1845, after which it steadily declined (see Appendix C). After payment of the dividend totalling £514 10s sufficient money remained to repair the Eardisley weighing-machine and the door to the machine-house.

The company's Act provided that should the company fail to fence any part of their line, or to keep the fences in repair, the owner of the land where this occurred was to be at liberty to make or repair the fence at the expense of the company who were to be liable for any future repairs or renewals.

When the Parliamentary line through the Moor (Lynhales) estate had been revised in 1818 the tramroad had been carried closer to the house than was originally proposed. To screen the tramroad from the house it had been agreed that the owner, J. Lloyd Harris, should be paid £30 by the company and £10 by Hazledine & Sayce to cover the cost of a small plantation. Later Harris entered into a private agreement with Sayce that the latter should plant hawthorn quicks on either side of the tramroad where it passed through the estate, and the fences and gates were maintained by Harris until his death in 1824.

The estate then passed to William Symonds who continued to maintain the fences and whose agent made improvements by planting blackthorn quicks to thicken the fences. The company's foreman, Daniel Daniel, also effected improvements by planting additional blackthorns at no cost to Symonds, but this was the limit of the company's interest in maintenance.

By 1840 the Moor estate had come into the hands of Charles William Allen. He wrote to the company on 22 January 1840 claiming ownership of a tree that the company considered stood on land which they had purchased at the time the line was constructed. In a further letter dated 7 February Allen required the company to repair the fences through the estate. In their reply the company stated that they did not consider it to be their liability and that Allen was free to make the fence in accordance with his own ideas but not at their expense.

There matters rested until 13 April 1842 when the company Clerk was served with a notice by Allen requiring the company to repair the fences. It was signed by two Justices of the Peace and had

been obtained by Allen without the company having had the opportunity of entering a defence. The company took no action and Allen did the necessary work. On 19 January 1844 the company was served with a notice signed by the same two Justices demanding that he be paid £37 11s 4d. The company maintained that an adequate fence could have been made for £15 7s.

On 16 April Allen commenced an action against the company which at first it was decided to defend. In July the company suggested that the matter should be settled by arbitration, but Allen would have nothing to do with such a settlement, and the *Hereford Journal* of 21 August published a somewhat scurrilous letter from him accusing the company of failure to comply with its Act. The company replied with a letter to the paper published on 11 September which described Allen's letter as angry, intemperate, bitter, discreditable and a perversion of the case, and contained a history of the part of the line concerned, denying that when the fences had been strengthened by Symonds and Daniel in 1836 the company had undertaken the responsibility for future repairs.

The case went against the company, largely on the grounds that J. Lloyd Harris had left nothing in writing that could bind his successors in title, and the company had to pay. On 17 June 1845 it was resolved to pay Richard Banks his law bill of £57 1s 'as soon as there are funds in hand to pay the same'.

The minutes contain very little information concerning the costs of maintaining the line. Hazledine & Sayce, and later Sayce on his own, received £186 per annum. As has been mentioned above, when Sayce gave up his contract there was a considerable decrease in the amount paid in this respect. Naturally the period from 1839 to 1845, when the company was at its most profitable, was also the time when traffic was at its greatest, and so was the wear and tear on the track. In December 1841 the proprietors authorised the payment of £132 to Meredith of Kington for plates, and more were obtained from J. and C. Bailey of Nantyglo Ironworks in 1848 at a cost of £83. From the regularly recurring entries in the minutes recording payments for 'blockstone' it appears that the stone obtainable locally was not particularly

60 *(above).* The Kington Railway adjacent to the wall of Lyonshall churchyard, climbing away from
the main road on a slight terrace. Lynhales lodge is visible in the background; and, 61 *(right),* the Kington
Railway as a balloonist above Lyonshall church might have seen it. The tramroad runs on a slight terrace below
the level of the churchyard, and across the main road between Leominster and Kington.
It then continues past Lynhales lodge and into Lynhales, or The Moor, estate.
Photo: Stephen K. Jones (1994) Drawing: Edward Paget-Tomlinson

suitable for this purpose. However, its use seems
to have continued, probably because it was the
most readily available. It is possible that the
breakage of plates was caused by failure of the
stone blocks.

In 1846, as has frequently been the case in the
face of declining profits, maintenance was the first
item to come under scrutiny and at the October
meeting the Clerk was instructed to 'procure
tramplates to an amount not exceeding £30 to be
used on such parts as most require them', with the
obvious intention that repairs should be effected
piecemeal. At the same time freighters in arrears of
their tonnages were to be sued should they fail to
pay within twenty-one days.

In common with the Hay Railway, the
Kington Railway was always very sensitive to the
price of coal, which comprised the bulk of the
upward traffic from Brecon. As early as January
1829 James Spencer, the Clerk to the Hay company, had warned the BBCO., the Brecon wholesalers, that Forest of Dean coal was being sold in
Kington, and unless they were prepared to reduce
their prices there was a danger of it finding its way
southward.[167] In October 1842 the Kington
Railway minuted that enquiries should be made of
the price at which the BBCO. would be prepared to
supply the company with coal, with the evident
intention of trading on their own account,
although this was not followed up. In December

E. W. R. T 5'95

of the same year Richard Parry, Sayce's partner in the coal trade, offered to reduce the price of household coal to 30s per ton at Kington if the tramroad would reduce its tonnages by ½d per ton per mile. The company deferred making a decision until efforts to obtain cheaper coal had been made.

Coal was clearly arriving at Kington in other ways than by tramroad, for in October 1844 the Kington Railway general meeting resolved that

... Mr. Sayce be requested to call upon the vendors of coal at Brecon when he goes there, for the purpose of endeavouring to prevail upon them to reduce the price of coal in order to prevent the reduction of demand from this country which must inevitably take place by reason of the new channels of supply at a lower rate than that of the Brecon coal.

The 'new channels of supply' are not named, but presumably it means that Staffordshire and Mamble coal carried along the Leominster Canal to Leominster and thence by road to Kington was affecting the market there. Heeding Spencer's warning, the resolution of 29 June 1829, which granted drawbacks on coal, lime and limestone, had been worded:

... provided that the said articles are not hauled on any part of the Turnpike Roads leading from Eardisley and from Lyonshall to Burlinjobb ...

in an endeavour to protect the Brecon trade from the competition of coal from the Forest of Dean and the Midlands. The former reached Kington

62. Gatepost cast at Meredith's foundry, Kington. The gate is close to Lyonshall church, across the Kington Railway at the point where it crossed the road from Leominster to Kington (A44). Photo: P. G. Rattenbury (1963)

by the present A4111 road, the latter by the present A44. Competition appears to have continued, however, and in October 1846 the dividend was reduced to £3 per share. This was repeated in 1847, but after that date dividends declined and in some years none was paid.

In an endeavour to stimulate trade, on 10 January 1849 it was decided to offer a drawback of ¾d per ton per mile on coal if the Hay company would reduce its rate by ¼d and the traders would undertake to sell best coal at Kington for 29s per ton. The other parties probably agreed to the conditions, for in the following November the Kington Railway offered to make a further reduction of ¼d if the Hay Railway would do the same – but there is no evidence that the later reductions took place. The January meeting also reduced all other tonnages by ½d per ton per mile without imposing any conditions.

The Hay company was also feeling the pinch and in January 1852 proposed that both companies and the B&A Canal should charge a flat rate of 1d per ton per mile on coal, but this was turned down by both the canal company and the Kington Railway.

The Shrewsbury & Hereford Railway was opened throughout on 6 December 1853, putting Leominster in direct contact with the industrial areas of Lancashire and the Midlands. The following January the Newport, Abergavenny & Hereford Railway was opened, forming a continuous line from Shrewsbury to Newport, Monmouthshire, and making the whole extent of the Monmouthshire coalfield available in competition with coal from the north Monmouthshire district which reached Kington via the B&A Canal and the Hay and Kington Railways.

Strenuous efforts continued to be made by the tramroad company to collect all outstanding tonnages, and in November 1853 William Bridgwater, the largest coal trader on the two tramroads, together with another unnamed trader, was sued for his debt. The Clerk was urged to impress on other traders the necessity of bringing their accounts up to date.

In March 1854 the Kington Railway proprietors were alarmed at the prospect of a railway being constructed to the town from Leominster, and a special meeting on 10 March considered a proposal that they should petition Parliament to reject the Leominster & Kington Railway Bill unless the L&K was disposed to purchase their tramroad. There were some at the meeting who thought that a railway connection would benefit the town and that a petition would be a waste of the company's money. The original motion in favour of a petition was carried by 68 votes to 27. By 23 March the idea of selling the tramroad to the railway company had gained support and it was resolved to appoint a delegation of three to confer with the L&K to see if terms could be arranged.

It appears that by this time 'foreign' coal was gaining ground in the district and the meeting of 23 March offered Bridgwater a further drawback of ½d per ton per mile 'if he will bona fide convey all his coals by the tramroad'. Bridgwater did not reply to the company's offer, and on 1 April the Clerk was instructed to inform him that 'in case no answer be forthwith given, the reduction will not take place'.

63. Commemorative ticket for the opening of the Leominster & Kington Railway, 27 July 1857.
Photo: C. R. Clinker collection, Brunel University Library

The possibility that the L&K Bill might not cover the purchase of the tramroad was discussed on 1 April, and it was decided to sound out the local representative of the railway company, a Mr John Cheese, to discover if there was any possibility of such powers being included. In response to a letter dated 6 April, three members were nominated to meet the L&K deputation on 13 April. Cheese attended the Kington Railway meeting on 1 May, when he announced that he intended to go to London to meet the L&K promoters. A letter from him was considered on 4 May from which it appears that the L&K was not in the least interested in purchasing the Kington Railway. It was resolved that 'this meeting is not prepared to make any new suggestion'. In the event the L&K Act of 10 July 1854 (17–18 Vic. c.144) did not give them the power to buy the tramroad.

The L&K was opened in mid-1857, and on 6 June the Kington Railway authorised the laying of a pipe alongside the tramroad from the pond serving Meredith's foundry to serve the railway's 'works', charging them 1s per annum for the privilege, the railway to effect any repairs. On 18 September a proposal from the L&K that a 'junction' should be made between the two companies was considered by the committee. This can only have been an interchange siding in view of the differing forms of track used by the two companies. From the agreement signed by David Wylie for the railway and by Richard Banks as chairman of the tramroad, as recorded in the minutes, it appears that the 'junction' took the form of a siding from the L&K running parallel with one from the Kington Railway, both running between stone walls with gates at either end, the whole construction to be at the cost of the railway company and to the satisfaction of the tramroad company.

The advent of the railway seems to have stimulated competition by the tramroad company as regards rates. On 18 September 1857 the latter reduced all its rates of tonnage to a flat 1½d per ton per mile on all cargoes. Nominally this was the same as was charged by the railway, but it must be remembered that the railway charge included ½d for the use of the company's trucks, whereas on the tramroad these had to be provided by the traders themselves.

It must have been painfully apparent to the proprietors that the days of the Kington Railway were numbered when early in 1857 Captain Walter Devereux, RN of Tregoyd, sowed the seeds of what later became the Hereford, Hay & Brecon Railway which superseded the Hay Railway in 1860.[168] It was evident that the coal trade with Brecon would, in the natural course of events, be killed as far as the tramroad was concerned, and the Kington company seems to have concentrated on developing the lime and limestone trade on their Burlinjobb line. There would be a fair demand for these products at places between Kington and Leominster and they could be passed over to the HH&B for onward transport southwards.

In November 1857 a new weighing-machine for the Kington depot was ordered through Meredith who was to erect it as soon as possible after receipt. In January 1860 Price, the Clerk, was ordered to advertise for 'a person to superintend the weighing-machine'. Two sites at the Sunset wharf were let to Henry Webb at £6 6s per annum, and John Morgan, described as a coal dealer, took five of the remaining sites at £12 per annum, both traders being given free use of the weighing-machine for all goods received or despatched along the tramroad with a charge of 2d per ton for goods despatched otherwise. One lot was reserved to the company for an extension to the machine-house, and the engagement of a machine-clerk was deferred until the possibility of erecting a residence for him had been investigated.

On 14 April 1858 the Clerk was authorised to sign a contract for the building of a house for the machine-clerk, and was instructed to re-advertise the position. William Pearce was appointed on 3 May at a weekly salary of 6s and was allowed an additional 2s per week until the house should be ready for his occupation. He was reminded that it was a tied house and would have to be vacated on his leaving the company's service.

Sundry small debts were written off at the meeting on 14 June, including 1s 3d due from 'The late Mr. M. Sayce', £4 19s 7d from 'The late Mr. James Davies', 9s 7d from the executors of John Cheese, and 8s 9d from 'The late Mr. Thomas Powell'. The largest amount shown was £9 11s 3d owed by the Kington Coal Co. The Clerk was instructed to collect all tonnages due to the previous 31 March 'and if necessary to instruct the solicitor'. A month later it was resolved that should Bridgwater fail to pay by 21 July proceedings should be started against him. It appears that he failed to pay his dues, and on 6 December he was given ten days to pay or be sued.

An increase in the lime and limestone trade is indicated by the order given on 25 October 1859 for an additional passing place to be inserted at Stanner, and the number of references in the minutes to orders for tramplates shows that maintenance was still a consideration.

The Kington Railway's worst fears were realised when the Act authorising the HH&B to purchase the Hay Railway was passed on 6 August 1860 (23–4 Vic. c.179). This would cut off their through-link to Brecon. The fact that the railway company was to retain railed communication with a point 'Three furlongs South-Eastward of Hay Bridge' and with Brecon, which had been inserted by the efforts of the B&A Canal, was no consolation, and on 5 November 1860 a request was forwarded to the HH&B that they should permit trams from the Kington Railway 'to pass to and from Eardisley Wharf ... from the termination of the Kington Tramroad ... a distance of 400 yards or thereabouts', the additional 200 yards being required to reach the Eardisley station of the HH&B from the original terminus of the Hay Railway.

On 19 November 1861 the Kington Railway proprietors met to consider an offer to purchase the tramroad that had been received from W. L. Banks, the Secretary of the HH&B. He offered shareholders £40 cash for each Kington Railway share, or £60 in shares in a new company which

64. The Kington Railway to the west of the church at Kington on the south bank of the Back Brook, photographed towards the end of its existence, probably no later than around 1870. By permission of Mrs E. H. T. Ridger and Hereford & Worcester County Record Office (Hereford)

would construct a locomotive railway from Eardisley to Kington, utilising such parts of the tramroad as were suitable, with a branch from Lyonshall to the L&K. It was proposed that the tramroad from Kington to Burlinjobb should be altered to 'a horse-railway on the narrow gauge'. It was resolved to call a general meeting for 19 December to consider the proposals. It is not known whether Banks was acting in a personal capacity or as agent for the HH&B. If the latter, it was probably thought that the ownership of the connecting line at Eardisley was a strong inducement for the Kington Railway to accept the offer.

By 19 December the position had changed and an offer was received from Thomas Savin, acting for the proposed Kington & Eardisley Railway which was to seek Parliamentary sanction in the coming Session, of £45 in cash or £60 in shares in the new company for each £100 Kington Railway share. It was resolved to accept the new offer by a majority of thirteen to one. On 6 March

1862 it was resolved to fix the common seal of the tramroad to a petition in favour of the K&E. Apparently the new company did not propose to convert the line from Kington to Burlinjobb, and the Kington Railway's Clerk was instructed to write to W. L. Banks, in his capacity as Secretary to the HH&B, to enquire if that company would be prepared to sell the tramroad three tons of plates!

The Kington Railway's 'Wharncliffe Meeting', held on 19 April 1862, unanimously approved of the sale, and ordered that the company's seal should be affixed to the Bill as evidence of the resolution.

The K&E obtained its Act on 30 June 1862 (25–26 Vic. c.67). This authorised the purchase of the Kington Railway and the use of such parts of the tramroad as were required to make a railway from a junction with the HH&B at Eardisley to a junction with the L&K at a point 'on the Kington side of the tenth mile-post from Leominster' at Titley Junction (SO 325582). The K&E was not to discontinue the use of the tramroad from Kington

65. The building in Kington which was used for meetings of the Kington Railway later in its history.
The entrance to Meredith's foundry is on the left of the notice board advertising Kington Economy Laundry.
The Kington Railway ran alongside the foundry wall behind the brick-built structure.
Photo: R. A. Cook (1958)

to Burlinjobb, which was to be fully maintained. The Schedule of the Act set out the terms of the sale contract under which the Kington Railway shareholders were to receive their payment by 30 September 1863, after which date outstanding amounts were to receive interest at 4 per cent per annum; but in this event the railway company was to receive any profits made by the tramroad. Further clauses specified that the railway company was to pay all expenses of the transfer and that the Clerk to the Kington Railway was to receive £50 per annum for life as compensation for loss of office, but was to continue to act as local agent for the K&E. The agreement was signed by Thomas Savin for the railway and by twenty-one Kington Railway shareholders either in person or by proxy.

The Act authorised the company to raise capital of £100,000 in shares of £10 each and to borrow £33,000. As the railway was not to follow the line of the tramroad for much of the way, additional land had to be purchased within three years of the passage of the Act, and five years were allowed for the completion of the works. Only from SO 32725195 (near Oldcastle) to SO 33005485 (where the tramroad turned north-westward to enter the grounds of Lynhales) did the route of the tramroad and the railway coincide, a distance of about 2¼ miles, which left the railway company to purchase land for about 4¾ miles of their line, a surface area of about 5¼ acres.

In their report to the shareholders at the half-yearly meeting on 24 February 1863, the directors of the K&E stated that subscriptions received amounted to £14,756 of which all but £236 had been spent. The purchase of the tramroad had been completed, but the cost was not revealed and it is not known how many of the tramroad shareholders had accepted shares in the railway and how many had chosen to be paid in cash.[169]

The optimistic report usual on such occasions was given at the next meeting on 18 August, when it was stated that the railway had been formed at Eardisley and some track had been laid. The 'engineers', Messrs Piercy, were making arrange-

106

66. Kington Railway cutting to the east of Elsdon, facing the direction of Lynhales.
At this point the Kington Railway was carried in a shallow cutting (shown here with a dense growth of trees) and then made a sharp right-angled turn to the south-west towards Eardisley (to the left in the picture). When the Kington & Eardisley Railway was constructed in 1868 the route from Eardisley continued straight on at this point in order to avoid the sharp bend in the Kington Railway. The ungrassed bank marks the boundary of the K&ER, broken by the abandoned Kington Railway cutting.
Photo: P. G. Rattenbury (1963)

ments to proceed with the next four miles, and it was anticipated that the entire line would be in progress shortly. It was thought that to achieve its full potential the company should set its sights on a terminus further north than Titley.[170]

A year later the report was a little more sombre, stating that during the last half year 'the works had not progressed to any considerable extent'. An Act had been obtained (27–28 Vic. c.199) for a branch from the L&K to Presteign, a distance of 7¼ miles, of which 1¼ miles was to be over L&K rails. To cover the cost of this, the capital might be increased by £90,000 and the borrowing by £30,0000.[171]

Applications for shares were being received only slowly, and at a special meeting on 6 January 1865 it was proposed that £50,000 of the capital authorised should be converted to 6 per cent preference shares,[172] and on 26 May assent was given to an Act (28–29 Vic. c.44) authorising this measure and also the issue of half shares. By 30 June 1865 only £35,974 had been received.[173]

A blow that might easily have been mortal to the company fell in 1866 when the contractor, Thomas Savin, failed. *Bradshaw's Railway Manual* for 1867 reported that as a consequence no accounts would be issued for 1866.

It was reported to the half-yearly meeting in February 1868 that the previous May a Mr J. Evans had undertaken the construction of the line to Lyonshall and that construction was now proceeding vigorously over the whole of the section. It had, however, been decided that savings could be effected if deviations were made in the line from Lyonshall to Titley and in the Presteign branch, and a Bill was to be introduced in the present Session to obtain the necessary authority.[174] The desired deviations were sanc-

67. Floodgates, Kington, facing east.
The K&ER extension from Kington to New Radnor passes over the level crossing. The earlier Kington Railway
ran in front of the cottages on the left of the picture and continued on the line of the curving track
towards Floodgates Mill (the white house in the background).
Photo: R&CHS (Bertram Baxter collection) (1952)

68. Floodgates, Kington. A similar view to that on the left, but taken about twenty-five years later. The K&ER line from Kington to New Radnor can just be identified as an overgrown strip of land with wire fencing on either side. The route of the Kington Railway is rather easier to distinguish as it passes in front of the cottages and follows the curving track towards the mill. The Kington by-pass road has subsequently been built on the line. The cottages have also been demolished.
Photo: P. G. Rattenbury (1976)

tioned on 13 July 1868, together with an extension by one year of the compulsory land purchase powers, and an extension to 1871 for completion. The Act (31–32 Vic. c.107) also granted the K&E running powers over the L&K from Titley to Kington and from Titley to the proposed Presteign branch. To February 1868 the capital account showed receipts of £53,036 of which £52,971 had been spent.

In its issue of 1869 *Bradshaw's Railway Manual* reported that the line was in abeyance, and that application was to be made to abandon certain parts of it and to extend the time for completion of the rest. The portion to be abandoned would appear to have been the Presteign branch, as under 34–35 Vic. c.186 the powers to construct

were given to the L&K. In the same Session the K&E were authorised to abandon the line and to extinguish the £90,000 capital authorised for its construction. They were also authorised to cancel £30,000 of their unissued shares and in their place to issue £20,000 debenture stock. The periods for land purchase and for completion of the railway were extended by one year and two years respectively.[175]

The company still had expansionist ideas, and in 1873 obtained an Act to construct a railway from Kington to New Radnor (36–37 Vic. c.79), but were forbidden to discontinue the tramroad to Burlinjobb until such time as the railway between the two places should be operational. To cover the cost of the extension they were granted additional capital of £60,000 and their borrowing powers were increased by £20,000. The time for completion of the line from Eardisley to Titley was extended by one year to June 1874.

In August 1873 it was reported that the line from Eardisley to Titley was progressing steadily, and that part of it was being made ready for for Government inspection, which it was hoped would be at an early date. Despite strong opposition from the HH&B full powers to run into and to use Eardisley station had been obtained and arrangements had been made with the Great Western Railway, who already worked the L&K, to work the K&E as well.[176] The K&E was opened on 3 August 1874 from Eardisley to Titley.

The 1873 report stated that Charles Chambers had been granted the contract for the railway to New Radnor, which it was hoped would be finished in the summer of 1874. Financial difficulties again appeared, and the financial statement to June 1875 showed that to date railways had cost £229,371 against capital receipts of £206,773 – a shortfall of £22,598.[177] To adjust the position the company again sought Parliamentary help and on 19 July 1875 sanction was given to an Act authorising them to increase their capital by the issue of £30,000 in £10 shares, and once that had been accomplished to borrow £10,000 on mortgage of the company.

The extension from Kington to New Radnor was opened on 25 September 1875, following a number of altercations with the Board of Trade before the carriage of passengers was sanctioned.[178]

The alacrity with which the tramroad management accepted the offer of purchase by the K&E in December 1861 is fair evidence that the Kington Railway's fortunes had been seriously affected by

the advent of the L&K, and with the exception of the four miles from Burlinjobb to Kington it is doubtful whether a profitable traffic could have been maintained. It is not known how long the tramroad from Eardisley to Kington remained in use after the takeover by the railway company. As has been mentioned above, very little of the railway route coincided with that of the tramroad, and whilst initially it may have been used to convey materials to Gipsy Hall or to Lyonshall, once the contractors had laid their temporary track its usefulness would have ceased.

No accounts for the K&E prior to 1867 have been found, but one ledger covering the period 1867–71 contains an account headed 'Kington Tramroad', which shows net receipts from the tramroad during this period, and it would appear that this is a summary of a separate set of books. There is only one debit entry – on 31 December 1871 the tramroad account is charged £20 in respect of 'Interest on Loan', indicating that the tramroad was, for accounting purposes, regarded as a separate entity.[179] The only other entries in respect of the tramroad appear in the K&E cash book showing that on 7 September and 16 October 1875 £600 and £350 was received from a J. Payne in respect of tramplates.[180] The quantity of plates disposed of to this gentleman is not specified. If it was only those in use from Kington to Burlinjobb the price paid would have been around £3 per ton, but if plates from the whole of the tramroad were involved it would have been considerably less per ton.

No wages or salaries accounts have been found, and it has not been possible to ascertain how long Thomas Price, the former tramroad Clerk, held his office under railway auspices.

Maps of
the Hay and Kington
Railways

A series drawn
by Ray Cook

Introduction to the Maps

THE maps which are reproduced on the following pages were originally drawn by Ray Cook in 1977. They were taken from the 1:63360 Ordnance Survey maps. The topographical features and annotations appear to derive from his exploration of the Hay Railway in the company of C. R. Clinker in preparation for the latter's study of the line. The maps were subsequently revised by Cook in 1986 to include additional topographical detail supplied by Gordon Rattenbury and to update some of the original information.

The maps are therefore in the state to which they were brought in 1986. Developments since then, notably in the form of road construction or realignment, are not shown. Rather than have a different cartographer modify Cook's work, and so detract from its integrity, the Publications Committee of the R&CHS has decided to publish them in the form in which he left them. Readers who wish to use the maps to follow the line of the tramroads should therefore bear in mind that they may no longer correspond exactly to arrangements on the ground.

The most obvious alterations have been brought about by four road improvement schemes. At Brecon a new by-pass runs to the south and east of the town: there is a large roundabout at Brynich bridge from which a realigned A470 road runs north more or less on the line proposed for the Hay Railway by Crosley in 1810. In Talgarth a new road has been built on the line of the Mid Wales Railway to the west of the town centre.

On the Kington Railway, at Kington itself a new by-pass has been built to the north of the town on the line of the Kington & Eardisley Railway. This has not affected the remains of the tramroad except where it crossed from the south to the north side of the river Arrow at Floodgates. Finally, from Stanner Rocks to Burlinjobb the B4594 road has been diverted, again onto the K&ER. The original road through Burlinjobb which is shown on Cook's maps remains but is only used for local purposes.

Needless to say, all the locomotive railways shown by Cook have long since been closed and the stations demolished or converted to other purposes.

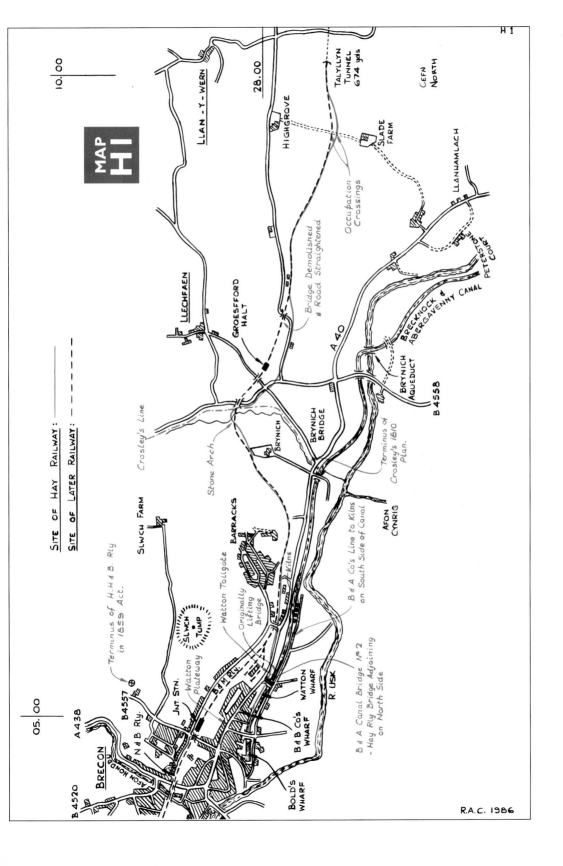

05.00

10.00

28.00

SITE OF HAY RAILWAY:

SITE OF LATER RAILWAY: – – – – – –

MAP
H1

LLAN - Y - WERN

HIGHGROVE

TALYLLYN
TUNNEL
674 yds

CEFN
NORTH

SLADE
FARM

Occupation
Crossings

LLANHAMLACH

PETERSTONE
COURT

BRECKNOCK &
ABERGAVENNY CANAL

B 4558

BRYNICH
AQUEDUCT

Terminus of
Crosley's 1810
Plan.

AFON
CYNRIG

BRYNICH
BRIDGE

BRYNICH

Bridge Demolished
& Road Straightened

A 40

LECHFAEN

GROESFFORD
HALT

Crosley's Line

Stone Arch

SLWCH FARM

Terminus of H.H & B. Rly
in 1859 Act.

BARRACKS

Watton Tollgate

Kilns

Bd A Co's Line to Kilns
on South Side of Canal

BRECON

B 4520

A 438

B 4557

N & B Rly.

AFON HONDDU

Jnt STN.

Watton Plateway

SLWCH
TUMP

Originally
Lifting Bridge

B&M RLY.

WATTON
WHARF

B & B Co's WHARF

R. USK

Bd A Canal Bridge Nº 2
- Hay Rly Bridge Adjoining
on North Side

BOLD'S
WHARF

R.A.C. 1986

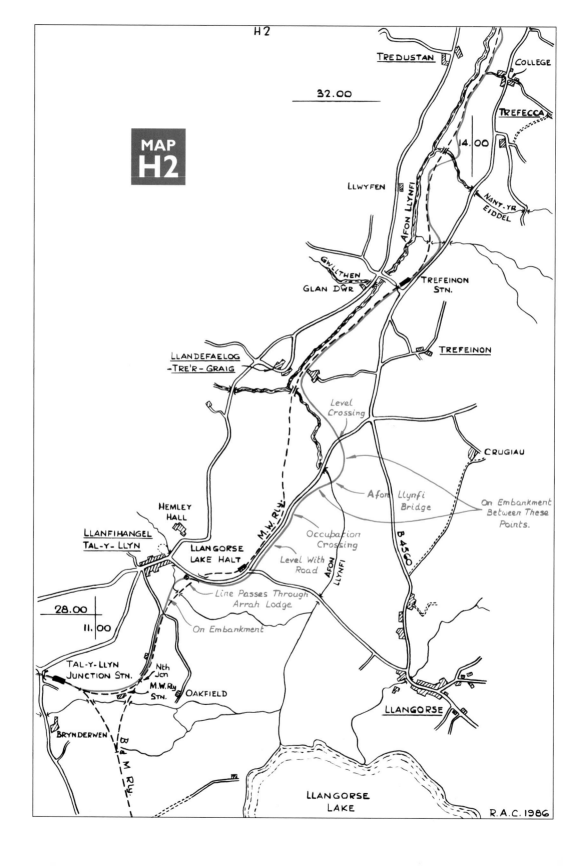

MAP
H2

32.00

14.00

TREDUSTAN

COLLEGE

TREFECCA

LLWYFEN

NANT-YR-EIDDEL

AFON LLYNFI

GWLITHEN

GLAN DWR

TREFEINON STN.

TREFEINON

LLANDEFAELOG
-TRE'R-GRAIG

Level Crossing

CRUGIAU

HEMLEY HALL

Afon Llynfi Bridge

On Embankment Between These Points.

LLANFIHANGEL
TAL-Y-LLYN

M.W.Rly.

LLANGORSE LAKE HALT

Occupation Crossing

Level With Road

AFON LLYNFI

B.4560

28.00

11.00

Line Passes Through Arrah Lodge

On Embankment

TAL-Y-LLYN JUNCTION STN.

Nth Jcn

M.W.Rly. STN.

OAKFIELD

LLANGORSE

BRYNDERWEN

B & M Rly.

LLANGORSE LAKE

R.A.C. 1986

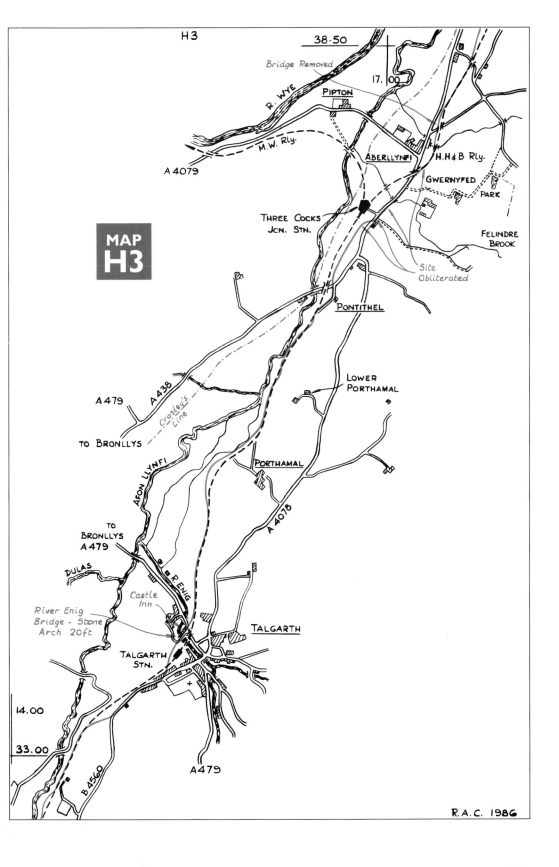

MAP
H3

H3

38·50

Bridge Removed

17. 00

R. WYE

PIPTON

M.W. Rly.

A 4079

ABERLLYNFI

H.H & B Rly.

GWERNYFED

PARK

THREE COCKS
JCN. STN.

FELINDRE
BROOK

Site
Obliterated

PONTITHEL

LOWER
PORTHAMAL

A 479

A 438

Crosley's
Line

TO BRONLLYS

PORTHAMAL

AFON LLYNFI

A 4078

TO
BRONLLYS
A 479

DULAS

R. ENIG

Castle
Inn

River Enig
Bridge - Stone
Arch 20ft

TALGARTH

TALGARTH
STN.

14.00

33.00

B 4560

A479

R.A.C. 1986

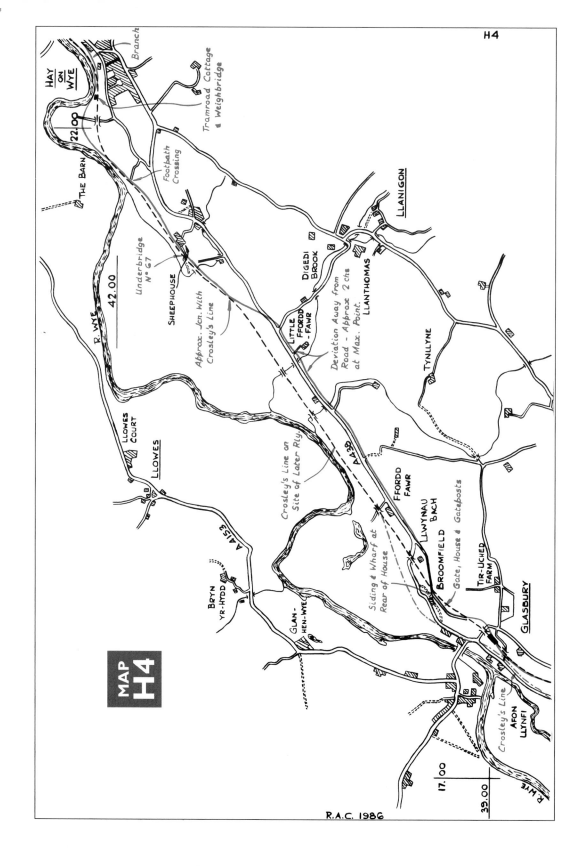

R.A.C. 1986

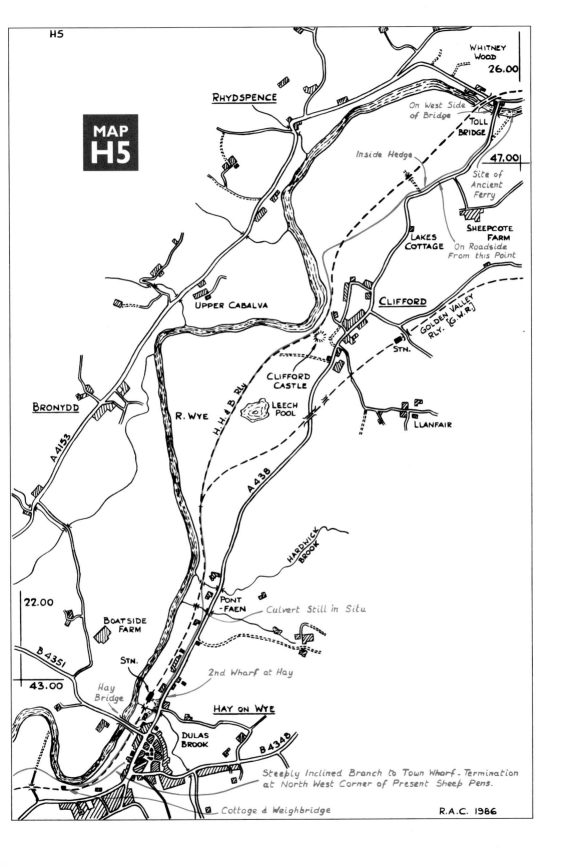

MAP
H5

WHITNEY
WOOD
26.00

RHYDSPENCE

On West Side
of Bridge

TOLL
BRIDGE

Inside Hedge

47.00

Site of
Ancient
Ferry

LAKES
COTTAGE

SHEEPCOTE
FARM
On Roadside
From this Point

UPPER CABALVA

CLIFFORD

GOLDEN VALLEY
RLY. [G.W.R.]

STN.

CLIFFORD
CASTLE

LEECH
POOL

LLANFAIR

BRONYDD

R. WYE

H.H.&B. Rly.

A 4153

A 438

HARDWICK
BROOK

22.00

BOATSIDE
FARM

PONT
-FAEN

Culvert Still in Situ

B 4351

STN.

43.00

*Hay
Bridge*

2nd Wharf at Hay

HAY ON WYE

DULAS
BROOK

B 4348

*Steeply Inclined Branch to Town Wharf - Termination
at North West Corner of Present Sheep Pens.*

▨ *Cottage & Weighbridge*

R.A.C. 1986

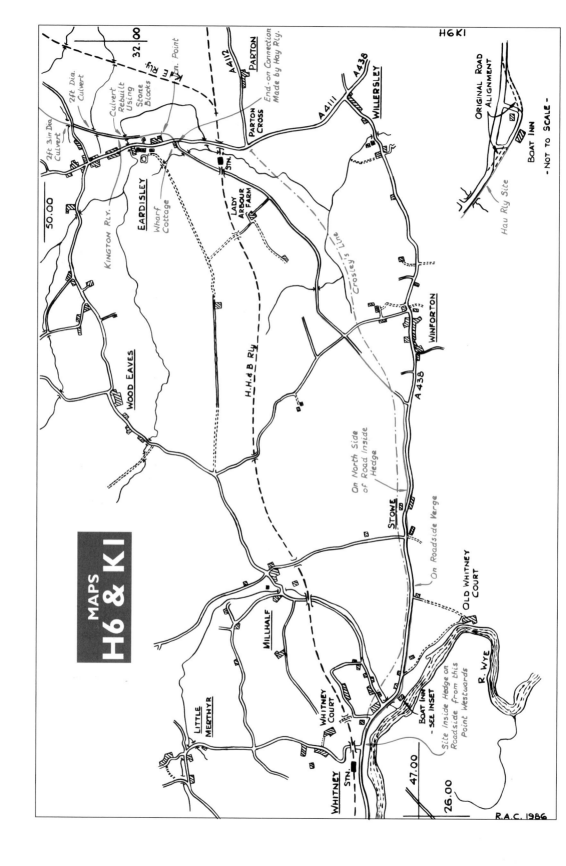

MAPS
H6 & KI

HGKI

32.00

50.00

2ft 3in Dia Culvert

2ft Dia. Culvert

Culvert Rebuilt Using Stone Blocks

Jun. Point

Hay Rly.

Kington Rly.

EARDISLEY

Wharf Cottage

WOOD EAVES

A4112

PARTON

PARTON CROSS

End-on Connection Made by Hay Rly.

A438

A4111

WILLERSLEY

A438

STN.

LADY ARBOUR FARM

Crosley's Line

WINFORTON

H.H.& B Rly

A438

On North Side of Road Inside Hedge

STOWE

On Roadside Verge

OLD WHITNEY COURT

LITTLE MEERTHYR

MILLHALF

WHITNEY COURT

BOAT INN - SEE INSET

Site inside Hedge on Roadside from this Point Westwards

R. WYE

WHITNEY

STN.

47.00

26.00

ORIGINAL ROAD ALIGNMENT

BOAT INN

- NOT TO SCALE -

Hay Rly Site

R.A.C. 1986

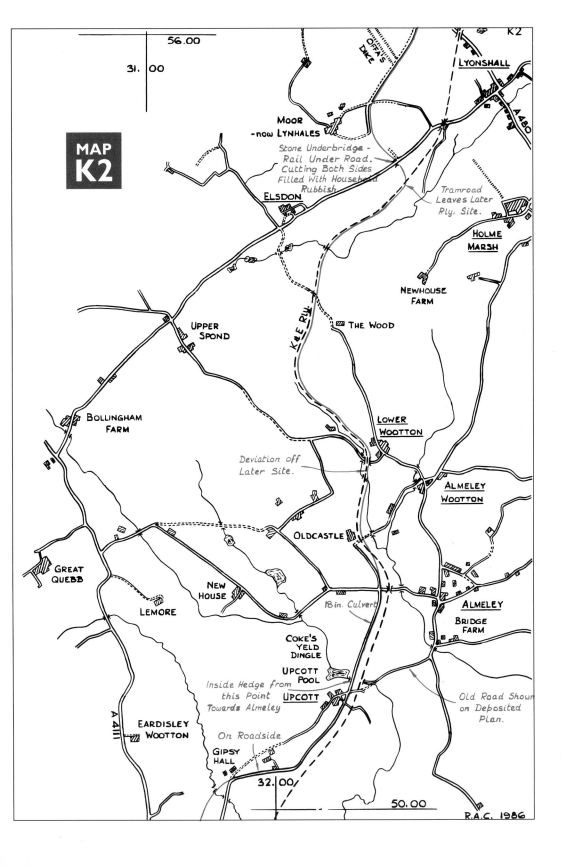

MAP
K2

56.00

31.00

K2

OFFA'S DYKE

LYONSHALL

A480

**MOOR
-now LYNHALES**

Stone Underbridge -
Rail Under Road.
Cutting Both Sides
Filled With Household
Rubbish

Tramroad
Leaves Later
Rly. Site.

ELSDON

**HOLME
MARSH**

**NEWHOUSE
FARM**

K&E Rly.

**UPPER
SPOND**

THE WOOD

**BOLLINGHAM
FARM**

**LOWER
WOOTTON**

Deviation off
Later Site.

**ALMELEY
WOOTTON**

**GREAT
QUEBB**

OLDCASTLE

**NEW
HOUSE**

18 in. Culvert

ALMELEY

LEMORE

**BRIDGE
FARM**

**COKE'S
YELD
DINGLE**

Inside Hedge from
this Point
Towards Almeley

**UPCOTT
POOL**

UPCOTT

Old Road Shown
on Deposited
Plan.

A 4111

On Roadside

**EARDISLEY
WOOTTON**

**GIPSY
HALL**

32.00

50.00

R.A.C. 1986

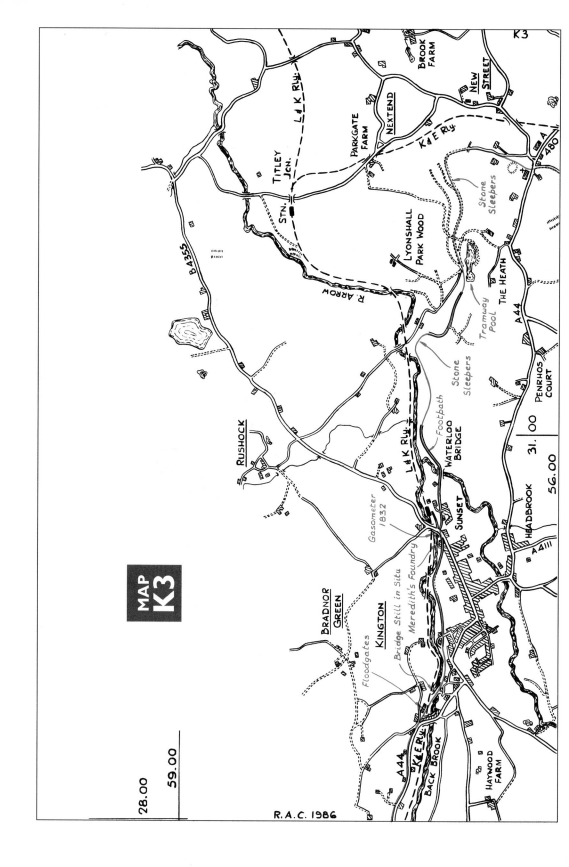

MAP
K3

K3

28.00
59.00

R.A.C. 1986

BRADNOR GREEN

RUSHOCK

B4355

KINGTON

Bridge Still in Situ

Meredith's Foundry

Floodgates

Gasometer 1832

L&K Rly.

SUNSET

WATERLOO BRIDGE

Footpath

Stone Sleepers

TITLEY JCN.

STN.

L&K Rly.

R. ARROW

LYONSHALL PARK WOOD

PARKGATE FARM

NEXTEND

K&E Rly.

Stone Sleepers

BROOK FARM

NEW STREET

A480

THE HEATH

Tramway Pool

A44

PENRHOS COURT

31.00

56.00

HEADBROOK

A4111

BACK BROOK

A44

K&E Rly.

HAYWOOD FARM

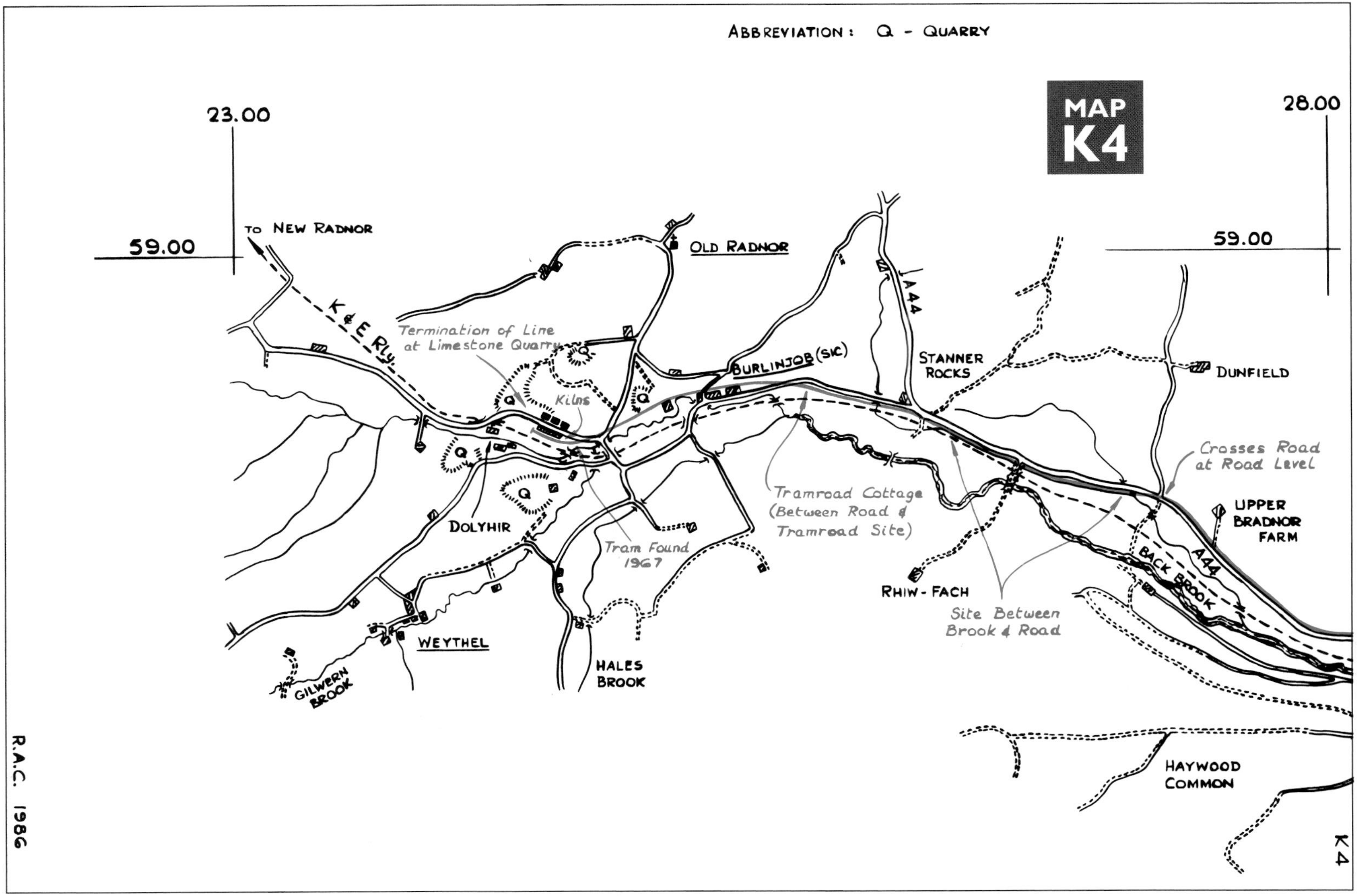

ABBREVIATION: Q - QUARRY

MAP K4

28.00
59.00
23.00
59.00

TO NEW RADNOR

K & E Rly.

Termination of Line
at Limestone Quarry

OLD RADNOR

Kilns

Tram Found
1967

DOLYHIR

HALES BROOK

WEYTHEL

GILWERN BROOK

BURLINJOB (Sic)

A44

STANNER ROCKS

Tramroad Cottage
(Between Road &
Tramroad Site)

RHIM-FACH

Site Between
Brook & Road

DUNFIELD

Crosses Road
at Road Level

UPPER BRADNOR FARM

A44

BACK BROOK

HAYWOOD COMMON

R.A.C. 1986

K4

Appendices

Subscribers to the Hay Railway Optional Loan

21 April 1815

Sir George Cornewall, Bart	£150
Sir Charles Morgan, Bart	(not stated)
Tomkyns Dew	150
John Morgan	30

21 November 1815

Walter Davies	£150

19 March 1816

Duke of Beaufort	£125
Marquess Camden	250
Earl of Ashburnham	250
Viscount Hereford	250
Hon. A. Foley, MP	125
Sir George Cornewall, Bart	250
Sir Charles Morgan, Bart, MP	875
Sir J. G. Cotterell, Bart, MP	125
Walter Wilkins, MP	500
T. F. Lewis, MP	250
Thomas Wood, MP	125
Thomas Foley	125
Samuel Peploe	500
Tomkyns Dew	250
George J. Cholmondley	125
Leonard Parkinson	125
Miss Bridget Hughes	50
John Morgan	50
Rev. William Parsons	25

11 December 1816

Walter Wilkins	£300
Umsdale Price	125
Robert Price	125
Thomas Wood	500
William Maddy	400
Tomkyns Dew	500
	£6,805

APPENDIX B
Kington Railway shareholders

Promoters (as shown in the Act)

Bebb, Joseph	£100
Banks, Richard [1]	100
Cheese, Edmund W. [2]	600
Cheese, John [2]	500
Clarke, John A. G.	200
Coke, Rev. Francis	100
Crummer, James [2]	1,000
Fencott, Elizabeth	300
Fletcher, John	100
Foley, Grace M.	200
Foley, Thomas	2,000
Harley, Frances	200
Harley, Martha	200
Harris, James L.	200
Hayward, Sarah	100
Hutchinson, Thomas	100
Jones, Rev. Thomas	100
Lewis, Percival	500
Mason, M.	100
Meredith, James W. [3]	100
Meredith, John [3]	300
Meredith, John (junior) [3]	100
Mitchell, John	300
Morris, John	1,500
Price, Richard	500
Romilly, Sir Samuel	500
Rogers, Henry	100
Rogers, Rev. John	200
Rogers, Thomas S.	300
Sherbourne, John	100
Symonds, William	200
Symonds, William (junior)	200
Sayce, Morris [4]	200
Watt, James [5]	500
Woolfe, Thomas	100
Total	£11,900

Received while Bill was in Parliament

Davies, James [2]	£1,000
Watt, James (junior)	500
Total	£13,400

Received before building started

Davies, H. P.	£100
Greenly, Mrs (Titley)	100
Harris, John	300
Lloyd, Thomas L.	100
Morgan, Sir Charles	200
Oxford, Earl of	100
Peel, Robert	200
Perry, C. Elizabeth	100
Perry, Thomas	300
Price, Robert	300
Stephens, James	200
Whittaker, Mrs John	100
Wilkins, Walter [6]	300
Total	£15,800

NOTES

1. Partner in Davies & Banks, solicitors to the company.

2. Partner in Kington & Radnorshire Bank, James Davies was treasurer to the company.

3. Ironfounders, Kington.

4. Surveyor, Kington, and contractor for the construction of the tramroad.

5. The pioneer steam-engine manufacturer. Partner in Boulton & Watt, Leeds. Retired to Doldowlod, Radnorshire, where he died in 1819.

6. Partners in Wilkins' Bank, Brecon

Appendix C

Summary of Kington Railway accounts as shown in the Minute Book

Date	Cash on Hand	Assets	Liabilities	Balance	Dividend
29.10.1832	—	—	—	—	2% (£294)
30.10.1838	—	—	—	—	3% (£441)
29.10.1839	£397	£1,106	£486	£620	3½% (£514 10s)
27.10.1840	367	1,191	613	578	3½%
26.10.1841	193	1,371	746	625	3½%
25.10.1842	—	—	—	—	3½%
31.10.1843	471	1,017	300	717	3½%
29.10.1844	320	903	305	598	3½%
28.10.1845	265	880	420	460	3½%
29.10.1846	3	783	325	458	3% (£441)
26.10.1847	103	880	368	512	3%
21.10.1848	313	867	539	327	2% (£294)
3.11.1849	380	808	449	359	2¼% (£330 15s)
29.10.1850	110	402	211	191	1½% (£220 10s)
28.10.1851	52	417	271	146	1% (£147)
26.10.1852	93	454	248	206	1½% (£220 10s)
1.4.1854 *	21	418	246	172	1% (£147)
31.10.1854	124	529	430	99	nil
20.11.1855	262	470	212	258	2% (£294)
28.10.1856	82	358	240	118	nil
7.10.1857	141	442	217	225	1½% (£220 10s)
26.10.1858	81	384	335	49	nil
25.10.1859	211	458	267	191	1% (£147)
5.11.1860	160	450	225	225	1½% (£220 10s)
19.11.1861	56	317	211	106	nil

* As at previous October

Appendix D

Biographical information

Brief biographical details of the main figures in the history of the Hay and Kingston Railways.

ALLEN, John and Hugh. Constructed part of the Hay Railway between Sheephouse and Pont Nichol Lane (1813–14). John was possibly the contractor who carried out remedial work on the roof of Talyllyn tunnel in 1817.

BAILEY, Joseph. Ironmaster and partner in Bailey & Wayne of Nantyglo Ironworks. Supplied tramplates to the Hay Railway (1811–13) and to the Kington Railway (1848).

BANKS, Richard. Solicitor to the Kington Railway and subsequently Chairman of the company. Partner in the Kington law establishment of Davies & Banks.

BOLD, Hugh. Brecon solicitor. Member of the committee of the B&A Canal. With his brother Thomas acted on behalf of the interests of Sir Charles Morgan (q.v.).

BRIDGWATER, William. Coal merchant of Glasbury and largest trader on both the Hay and Kington Railways. His stables at Llwynau Bach near Glasbury still survive.

CHEESE, John C. Clerk to the Kington Railway (1818–38).

COBB, J. R. Brecon solicitor and promoter with J. P. de Winton (q.v.) of the Brecon & Merthyr Railway.

CROSLEY, William. Engineer to the B&A. His initial survey of the Hay Railway in 1810 was authorised by the Act of Incorporation but subsequently modified by John Hodgkinson (q.v.).

DAVIES, David. Surveyor, of Llangattock. Valued the land required for the Hay Railway in Breconshire (1811).

DAVIES, James. Partner in the Kington & Radnorshire Bank. Treasurer of the Kington Railway from 1818.

DEVEREUX, Walter. Shareholder in the Hay Railway and promoter of the Hereford, Hay & Brecon Railway (1857).

DE WINTON, John Parry. Formerly Wilkins. Chairman of the Brecon & Merthyr Railway; promoter with John Cobb (q.v.) of the Brecon & Merthyr Railway.

DUNSFORD, William. Assisted Hodgkinson (q.v.) in supervising the construction of the Hay Railway (1811–4); appointed resident engineer in succession to Hodgkinson (1814–16).

ELLWOOD, Thomas. Mineral agent and general factotum of the BBCO. Author of a letter to the BBCO. in 1816 which described the state of the Hay Railway.

FRERE, Edward. Ironmaster and partner in Clydach Ironworks; member of B&A committee and of Hay Railway committee. Supplied tramplates to the Hay Railway (1811).

GAMES, John. Weighing-machine clerk at Hay (1824–31).

HAZLEDINE, William. Ironfounder of Shrewsbury. With M. Sayce (q.v.) constructed and maintained the Kington Railway (1818–32).

HODGKINSON, John. A major figure in tramroad development in south-east Wales and adjoining areas of England. Proposed a tramroad between Leominster and Kington (1803). Appointed engineer to Hay Railway and carried out re-survey (1811); supervised construction of Hay Railway until dismissed in 1814 for irregular attendance; held several contracts for construction of parts of the Hay Railway (1815–18) and for maintenance (until 1826). Prepared plans for the Kington Railway and tendered unsuccessfully for its construction (1818). Also engineer of Bullo Pill, Llanvihangel, Grosmont, Hereford and many other tramroads in the area. Died 1861 and is buried in the churchyard of St Woolos, Newport (now the cathedral).

JAMES, Thomas. Succeeded his partner, James Spencer (q.v.) as Clerk to the Hay Railway (1847) and remained in office until the dissolution of the company (1863).

JONES, John. Contractor of Abergavenny. Constructed part of Hay Railway in vicinity of Hay (1812–3) in partnership with John Williams (q.v.).

JONES, Stephen Bowen. Replaced Richard Oliver (q.v.) as 'Superintendent of the Line' of the Hay Railway (1831). Resigned at an unknown date but before 1850.

LLEWELLIN, John. Agent to Benjamin Hall of the Rhymney Ironworks. Supervised construction of Brinore Tramroad (1814–15). Reported on the state of the track of the Hay Railway (1819).

MORGAN, Sir Charles. 2nd baronet (1760–1846). Major landowner in the vicinity of Brecon and in Monmouthshire. Member of committee of Hay Railway to which he advanced loans totalling £875. Also a shareholder in the Kington Railway. The seat of the family was at Tredegar Park on the outskirts of Newport.

MURPHY, Peter. Contractor of Abergavenny. Constructed parts of Hay Railway in vicinity of Hay and Llangorse (1812–14).

OLIVER, Richard. Agent and Clerk to Hay Railway (1816). Assumed responsibility for maintenance after the end of Hodgkinson's contract (1826). By 1830 had taken over much financial management from Spencer (q.v.) including collection of tolls. Resigned in 1831.

OVERTON, George. Mining engineer and coal owner. Constructed Brinore Tramroad (1814–15) which he subsequently (1821) attempted to extend from Talybont on Usk to Llanvihangel Talyllyn where it would have joined the Hay Railway. Owned limekilns and quarries at Dolyhir and tendered unsuccessfully for construction of Kington Railway (1818). Major trader (via B&A) on Hay and Kington Railways. Died in 1827.

PERKS, Thomas Chandler. Weighing-machine clerk at Hay (1831). Appears to have succeeded S. B. Jones (q.v.) as Superintendent of the Line of the Hay Railway at some date before 1850. Additionally appointed Clerk of the Brinore Tramroad (1855).

POWELL, John. Brecon solicitor (Powell & Jones). Partner in BBCO. and promoter, with others of the Hay Railway.

PRICE, Thomas. Clerk to Kington Railway (1838).

RASTRICK, John Urpeth. Leading civil engineer. Advised Hay Railway on possible means of crossing the river Wye at Whitney (1818).

SAYCE, Morris. With Hazledine (q.v.) held contract for construction and maintenance of the Kington Railway (1818–32) and subsequently on his own (1832–3). Trader on Hay and Kington Railways (in partnership with Richard Parry).

SPENCER, James. Hay solicitor. Clerk and Solicitor to Hay Railway (1810–47). His financial responsibilities were gradually taken over by Oliver (q.v.) during later 1820s in view of irregularities in accounting on the part of Spencer. Imprisoned for debt in 1847 following irregularities in handling the moneys of a charitable foundation. Died in Hereford jail in 1851, aged 85.

THACKER, John. Contractor, with Anthony Tissington (q.v.), for construction of Hay Railway between Llanvihangel and Sheephouse (1812–13).

THOMAS, David. Brecon solicitor. Solicitor to Brinore Tramroad and promoter of Hereford, Hay & Brecon Railway.

TIPPING, Robert. Contractor for construction of Hay Railway between the Watton and Llanvihangel Talyllyn (1812).

TISSINGTON, Anthony. Contractor, with John Thacker (q.v.), for construction of Hay Railway between Llanvihangel and Sheephouse (1812–13).

WANEWRIGHT, Benjamin. Surveyor of Hereford. Valued land required by Hay Railway in Herefordshire (1811).

WILKINS, Jeffreys. Partner in Brecon Bank (bankers to B&A) and partner in BBCO. Promoter, with others, of Hay Railway. Banker to Hay Railway.

WILKINS, John Parry. Partner in Brecon Bank. Treasurer to Hay Railway (1812).

WILLIAMS, John. Contractor of Llanfoist. Held contract with John Jones (q.v.) for construction of Hay Railway in vicinity of Hay.

WILLIAMS, William. Partner in Brecon Bank. Treasurer of Hay Railway until his death in 1812.

REFERENCES

1. For the history of the Brecknock & Abergavenny Canal, *see* Charles Hadfield, *The Canals of South Wales and the Border*, 2nd ed. (Newton Abbot: David & Charles, 1967), pp.160–83

2. *Hereford Journal*, 12 June 1793

3. Brecknock Museum, Brecon. Maybery collection, vol.2, fo.51

4. Hadfield, *Canals of South Wales*, pp.163–4

5. Glamorgan Record Office, Cardiff. D/519/11/16

6. *Hereford Journal*, 1 August 1810

7. Brecknock Museum. Maybery collection, vol.1A, fo.17

8. Public Record Office, Kew. Brecknock & Abergavenny Canal committee minutes, 23 August 1810 (RAIL 812/4)

9. Hereford City Library. Local collection. For the original version of Crosley's plan, *see* Hereford & Worcester Record Office, Hereford. Q/RW/T1

10. National Library of Wales, Aberystwyth. Maybery 4094

11. PRO. B&A committee minutes, 18 December 1810 (RAIL 812/5)

12. NLW. Tredegar 45/178

13. *Hereford Journal*, 30 January 1811

14. NLW. Tredegar 49/8

15. John van Laun, 'The Hay Railway: the Passing of an Early Railway Act', *Journal of the Railway & Canal Historical Society*, vol. XXII, no.1, 1976, pp.2–10

16. NLW. Maybery 902

17. van Laun, 'Hay Railway'

18. NLW. Tredegar 45/182

19. Ibid. 45/183

20. van Laun, 'Hay Railway'

21. For Crosley's original plan (Brynich to Parton Cross), *see* H&WRO. Q/RW/T1. For his revised plan (showing both Brecon and Brynich as alternative termini), *see* H&WRO. Q/RW/T2. A third version of the plan, showing Brecon as the only terminus, is held in Hereford City Library

22. 51 Geo. III c.222

23. H&WRO. N44/1 (Hay Railway committee minutes). The proprietors' minutes do not appear to have survived

24. Hodgkinson had been the engineer to the Gloucester & Cheltenham Railway. See D. E. Bick, *The Gloucester and Cheltenham Railway* (South Godstone: Oakwood Press, 1969)

25. Hereford City Library. Printed copy of Hodgkinson's report

26. Joseph Priestley, *Historical Account of the Navigable Rivers, Canals and Railways throughout Great Britain* (Longman, etc., 1831), p.355

27. Hereford City Library. Hodgkinson's report

28. H&WRO. Q/RW/T1, T2 (Crosley); Q/RW/T3, T4; N44/2 (Hodgkinson)

29. NLW. Tredegar 45/212

30. van Laun, 'Hay Railway'

31. NLW. Maybery 4096

32. Ibid.

33. NLW. Tredegar 45/764

34. NLW. Tredegar 45/230. Italics are in the original

35. PRO. B&A committee minutes, 12 March 1812 (RAIL 812/5)

36. NLW. Tredegar 45/218

37. H&WRO. N44/1 (Hay Railway committee minute book which records in full the resolutions of the Hay Railway and of the canal committee)

38. 52 Geo. III c.115. van Laun, 'Hay Railway'

39. NLW. Tredegar 45/206

40. PRO. RAIL 500/43 (3)

41. H. W. Paar, *The Great Western Railway in Dean* (Newton Abbot: David & Charles, 1965), p.21

42. Paar, *Great Western Railway in Dean*, pp.141–3. *The Cambrian*, 21 November, 24 December 1812. *Hereford Journal*, 7 August 1811.

43. GRO. D/179

44. NLW. Tredegar 45/225

45. PRO. B&A committee minutes, 30 May 1811 (RAIL 812/5)

46. NLW. Tredegar 45/231

47. Gordon Rattenbury, *Tramroads of the Brecknock & Abergavenny Canal* (Oakham: Railway & Canal Historical Society, 1980), p.100

48. C. R. Clinker, *The Hay Railway* (Dawlish: David & Charles, 1960), p.40

49. Paar, *Great Western Railway in Dean*, p.22

50. The Llanvihangel Railway was opened from Govilon to Blaengavenny on 12 March 1814 (*Hereford Journal*, 13 April 1814)

51. Bank lending on the security of promissory notes was common practice, but usually on short-dated notes only

52. H&WRO. N44/1 (Hay Railway committee minutes, 21 April, 21 November 1815, 19 March, 11 December 1816

53. Ibid. 19 March 1816

54. Brecknock Museum. Maybery collection, vol.1, fo.43

55. Priestley, *Navigable Rivers*, p.355

56. *Hereford Journal*, 15 May 1816

57. Ibid. 22 May 1816

58. PRO. B&A committee minutes, 19 July 1816 (RAIL 812/6)

59. Brecknock Museum. Maybery collection, vol.1, fo.43

60. PRO. B&A committee minutes, 19 July 1816 (RAIL 812/6)

61. H&WRO. N44/1. *See also* G. L. Fairs, 'New Light on the Hay Railway', *Severn & Wye Review*, vol.1, no.3, 1971, pp.65–2. G. L. Fairs, 'Recent discoveries about the Hay Railway 1816–1868', *Transport History*, vol.10, no.1, 1979, pp.13–20

62. Grahame Boyes, 'The Exchequer Loan Commissioners as a Source of Canal and Railway Finance', *Journal of the Railway & Canal Historical Society*, vol. XXIV, no.3, 1978, pp.85–92

63. Clinker, *Hay Railway*, p.50 (note 56) states that Hodgkinson was paid £2,100. The figure of £2,400 has been obtained from the minute book by addition. The last payment recorded there on 8 August 1820 is stated to be 'on further account'. No final payment is recorded.

64. NLW. Maybery 6396

65. When Chepstow bridge was rebuilt in iron to Rastrick's design in 1816 a ferry was used to maintain passage over the river

66. NLW. Tredegar 121/815

67. Ibid. 121/816

68. H&WRO. Kington Railway minutes, 2 June 1818 (E/86)

69. Hereford City Library. Local collection

70. The Hay Railway minutes do not quote the date of opening. 11 December 1818 is given by F. B. Ellison, 'The Hay Railway 1810–1863', *Transactions of the Newcomen Society*, vol.XVIII, 1937/8, pp.29–42

71. Gordon Rattenbury, 'Hall's Tramroad', *Journal of the South East Wales Industrial Archaeology Society*, vol.III, no.1, 1978. Rattenbury, *Tramroads of the Brecknock & Abergavenny Canal*, p.120

72. Rattenbury, *Tramroads of the Brecknock & Abergavenny Canal*, pp.111, 126

73. Brecknock Museum. A29/2/3 (57)

74. George Overton, *A Description of the Faults or Dykes of the Mineral Basin of South Wales, Part I* (London: 1825). Part II does not appear to have been written

75. Clinker, *Hay Railway*, p.31

76. NLW. Maybery 1123
77. Brecknock Museum. Maybery collection, vol.2, fo.117
78. PRO. B&A proprietors' minutes, 19 October 1826 (RAIL 812/2)
79. Priestley, *Navigable Rivers*, pp.351–2 (Grosmont Railway), pp.360–1 (Hereford Railway), pp.228–30 (Duffryn Llynvi & Porth Cawl Railway). Gwent Record Office, Croesyceiliog. Q/P&BR 15, 22 (Llanvihangel Railway). Derbyshire Record Office, Derby. Gell/55/23B ('Section of the Cromford & High Peak Railway')
80. Waybills held in H&WRO (N44/5) show that waggons numbered 101–104 had a tare weight of 1 ton 4cwt each and carried a load of three tons compared to the tare weight of the remainder of 10–12cwt. A gross weight of over four tons would seem to be excessive for being carried on four wheels, but no record has been found to indicate a greater number of wheels or the use of bogeys
81. Clinker, *Hay Railway*, p.31–2
82. No copy of these accounts has been found
83. NLW. Maybery 3155
84. Ibid. 3162
85. Brecknock Museum. Maybery collection, vol.1, fo.99
86. H&WRO. N44/1
87. Brecknock Museum. Maybery collection, vol.1, fo.99
88. *Hereford Journal*, 23 December 1840
89. G. L. Fairs, *A History of the Hay* (Phillimore, 1972), p.268
90. A Member of the Mechanics Institute of Kington, 'A History of Kington' (n.d., *c*.1845) in the Pelley collection, Hereford Library
91. *Hereford Journal*, 13 September 1843; *Hereford Times*, 23 September 1843. Fairs, *Recent discoveries*
92. NLW. Tredegar 84/393
93. H&WRO. N44/1
94. *Hereford Journal*, 23 April 1845, published the prospectus of the company
95. NLW. Tredegar 84/362
96. Ibid. 84/363
97. Ibid. 84/363
98. *Hereford Journal*, 22 October 1845
99. Ibid., 25 March 1846
100. H&WRO. N44/1 (Introduction to the collection)
101. NLW. Maybery 6413
102. H&WRO. Kington Railway minutes, 3 November 1849 (E/86)
103. Ibid., 29 January 1852
104. PRO. B&A committee minutes, 29 January 1852 (RAIL 812/7)

105. Ibid., 27 April, 10 August 1854
106. Rattenbury, *Tramroads of the Brecknock & Abergavenny Canal*, pp.22–3
107. A successor to the original chairman of the the Hay Railway, who had died in 1843
108. *Hereford Journal*, 9 August 1854
109. Ibid., 27 September 1854
110. Ibid., 11 October 1854
111. Ibid., 1 November 1854
112. Ibid., 18 January 1837
113. Ibid., 25 March 1846
114. D. S. M. Barrie, *The Brecon & Merthyr Railway* (Lingfield: Oakwood Press, 1957), p.103
115. V. J. Parry, *Brecon & Merthyr Railway* (Brecon: priv. print., 1970), p.8
116. *Hereford Journal*, 1857–8 *passim*
117. Ibid., 12 May 1858
118. Ibid., 22 September 1859. *Hereford Times*, 9 March 1846 (letter from Capt. Devereux)
119. *Hereford Journal*, 2 March 1859
120. Ibid., 1 June, 8 June 1859
121. Ibid., 12 October 1859
122. Rex Christiansen & R. W. Miller, *The Cambrian Railways, Vol. I: 1852–1888* (Newton Abbot: David & Charles, 1967), p.108
123. *Hereford Journal*, 7 December 1859
124. Ibid., 16 November 1859
125. Ibid., 7 December 1859
126. Ibid., 8 February 1860
127. Ibid., 3 May 1860
128. Ibid., 16 May 1860
129. PRO. B&A committee minutes, 1 February 1860 (RAIL 812/7). NLW. Maybery 1050
130. NLW. Maybery 1051
131. PRO. B&A committee minutes, 1 February 1860 (RAIL 812/7)
132. Barrie, *Brecon & Merthyr Railway*, p.108
133. 23–24 Vic. c.65 (MWR). 24–5 Vic. c.235 (B&MR)
134. Clinker, *Hay Railway*, p. 45
135. Brecknock Museum. Maybery collection, vol.1, fo.99 (1823 accounts). H&WRO. N44/1 (1843 accounts)
136. John van Laun, 'Excavation on the Hay Railway', *Journal of the Railway & Canal Historical Society*, vol.XXIII, no.3, 1977, pp.83–6
137. Rattenbury, *Tramroads of the Brecknock & Abergavenny Canal*, p.126
138. E. H. Morris, 'The Abergavenny–Hereford Tramroads', Part 1, *Railway Magazine*, vol.93, 1947, pp.138–42
139. van Laun, 'Excavation on the Hay Railway'
140. Morris, 'The Abergavenny–Hereford Tramroads' (illustration)

141. Ellison, 'Hay Railway 1810–1863'
142. R. A. Cook, letter in *Journal of the Railway & Canal Historical Society*, vol.XXIV, no.1, 1978, p.36
143. Paar, *Great Western Railway in Dean*, p.33
144. H&WRO. N44/5
145. John van Laun, unpublished study of traffic on the Hay Railway
146. Ibid.
147. Ibid.
148. Overton, *Description of the Faults or Dykes*
149. For the history of the Leominster Canal, *see* Hadfield, *Canals of South Wales*, pp.191–8
150. 51 Geo. III c.122
151. 52 Geo. III c.106
152. NLW. Maybery 4094 ('Observations on the Hay Railway', accompanying William Crosley's plan of 1810)
153. NLW. Tredegar 121/817
154. Partners: James Davies, James Crummer, John Cheese, E. W. Cheese
155. H&WRO. E/86
156. H&WRO. N44/1
157. Brecknock Museum. Maybery collection, vol.1, fo.99 (Hay Railway accounts to 1823)
158. H&WRO. Kington Railway minutes, 5 November 1860 (E/86)
159. *Hereford Journal*, 22 March 1820
160. Ibid., 9 August 1820
161. Ibid., 19 September 1821
162. Clinker, *Hay Railway*, pp.56–60, publishes the 'Bye Laws, Orders, and Regulations' of the Hay Railway
163. Memorial in Llandetty church, near Brecon
164. By some error on the part of the Clerk this minute appears in the proprietors' minute book
165. A bushel contained eight gallons (dry measure), which is about the size of a petrol tank of a small car or a little over 1¼ cu. ft
166. *Hereford Journal*, 22 January, 29 January, 12 February, 2 March 1834
167. NLW. Maybery 3155
168. Clinker, *Hay Railway*, p.43
169. *The Times*, 25 February 1863
170. Ibid., 19 August 1863
171. Ibid., 29 August 1864
172. Ibid., 7 January 1865
173. *Bradshaw's Railway Manual, Shareholders' Guide and Directory*, 1866
174. *The Times*, 11 February 1868
175. *Bradshaw's Railway Manual*, 1872
176. Ibid., 1874
177. Ibid., 1876
178. PRO. MT 6/143-11
179. PRO. RAIL 336/13
180. PRO. RAIL 336/17, fo.31

INDEX